Father-Time Continuum

TÓSÌN AKỌMỌLÁFẸ

Published by The Invisible Imprint in the United Kingdom in 2023

ISBN: 978-1-83919-547-1

For Tàní

A note from the Author

I have tried to be as accurate as possible in my depiction of the real people and events that inspired this book. However, I have also taken creative liberties to create a more engaging and fictionalized story. I apologise if any of the characters or events in this book offend or harm anyone. This was not my intention. I hope you enjoy reading this book as much as I enjoyed writing it.

Prologue

In the aftermath of climate change, a student faced a dilemma – to fight the famine threatening farming or surrender to the allure of storytelling. Tòbí sat in his dorm room, lost in thought, staring blankly at his computer screen as if it held the secrets of the universe. He had always been conflicted between his passion for writing and the practicality of studying agricultural science. It was a degree in high demand, but Tòbí couldn't shake the feeling that he was meant to be doing something else. Something more. He was searching for inspiration when he went to visit his grandmother.

Her cosy home was a world away from the sterile halls of his university. As they sipped tea, she shared her father's old recordings with him. Tòbí was enthralled by the podcast format and his great-grandfather's captivating voice. He listened as the elder recounted his life's struggles and triumphs. Suddenly, an idea struck Tòbí, a wild and off-kilter idea that he couldn't shake.

"What if I transcribed these recordings into a book?" he blurted out to his grandmother.

She smiled and nodded in agreement. "That's a wonderful idea, Tòbí. Your great-grandfather had a gift for storytelling, and he always hoped to publish a book about his stories. He just never got around to doing it. You have my support."

Tòbí was enthusiastic, but soon doubts began to creep in. *What if I can't do the recordings justice? What if I fail?* His grandmother reassured him, telling him to have faith in his writing abilities.

Taking a deep breath, Tòbí resolved to transcribe the recordings into a book. He listened to each audio file, his imagination soaring as he immersed himself in the stories and vibrant voices captured by his great-grandfather. But it wasn't all smooth sailing. Some of the recordings were missing or damaged. Tòbí was ready to give up when a surprise package arrived in the mail, a set of old cassette tapes labelled with his great-grandfather's name. They were a gift from his grandmother, who had found them in her attic.

Tòbí's fingers flew over the keyboard as he transcribed each recording, pouring his heart and soul into the project, while of course keeping up with his school work. He felt overwhelming gratitude to his grandmother, who had given him the gift of his great-grandfather's voice and inspired him to rediscover his love for writing. He knew that his work would be a tribute to his family's legacy and a chance for others to hear the stories of their forebears. He titled it the *Father-Time Continuum*, a fitting tribute to his great-grandfather's legacy.

Act I: Childhood

"Born without a choice,
Existential thoughts arise,
Gratitude finds voice."
- Tòbí

Chapter 1

"Grandma?" I asked.

"Yes, darling?" she replied.

"Can I go buy some ice cream when the vendor comes on our street?"

"Yes, you can, Akándé. But be careful, and look both ways when you cross the road."

"I will. Thank you."

Thinking back to my childhood, most of my daily activities were a blur, but memories of ice cream, the school playground, and my family stuck with me. The things I did remember were fundamental to the man I would turn out to be. One of my earliest and fondest memories involved the neighbourhood ice cream man. Mr Bassey rode a flamboyant-looking tricycle with a large cooler on the back seat, and he played an entrancing ice cream jingle that had kids chasing after him, like he was the Pied Piper of frozen delights. I was one of those kids. He only had three flavours for sale: strawberry, chocolate, and vanilla. The chocolate flavour was my favourite, and judging by its popularity, it was other kids' favourite too. But it always ran out just before the ice cream vendor took a turn onto our street. Maybe I liked chocolate-flavoured ice cream because it was a rarity, or perhaps I only noticed its rarity because I liked it. Classic chicken-and-egg dilemma.

An act of faith came one day. I resolved in my mind that the next Saturday afternoon when the ice cream man came by, I would get a cone filled with scoops of creamy, frosted cocoa sweetness, melting on the top of my tongue with every slurp. I visualised it, and there was no denying me. I hoped and prayed, squeezing my money tight while peeking through the balcony at home, patiently waiting and watching from an ideal vantage point, good enough to spot the ice cream man as soon as he turned the corner into our buzzing Lagos Mainland street.

Even my grandpa came by to tease me, saying, "Don't you have something more important to—"

I interrupted him by jolting up at the blaring sound of the catchy ice cream jingle coming from down the road. I dashed past my grandpa out of the house, attempting to make a beeline through the clamouring street straight to the vendor. I hadn't even seen the ice cream man; all I needed was that auditory cue. As I ran past the front door, my mother and her younger sister, whom I affectionately called Aunty Mimi, said in sync, "Where are you running off to?"

"I'm just going to get some ice cream," I responded, pointing in the direction I was headed.

"Okay, be careful. And get one for me please!" my mum said.

"And me too," Aunty Mimi added, as I threw my hand up in acknowledgement. Both my mum and Aunty Mimi had a sweet tooth like no other, and we often indulged our sugar cravings, even though we all knew excess sugar was bad for oral hygiene and overall health.

Seeing as other kids were also coming out into the street, I made sure I got to the ice cream man quickly enough. I got to him panting, out of breath yet bursting with confidence, sweat streaming down my face. He parked his bike in a safe spot and, with his familiar stuttering lisp, asked, "What flavour d-d-do you want?"

"Three chocolate cones, please?" I requested with hopeful eyes, as I stood in front of the ice cream man. Beneath his horn-rimmed glasses, he had a furrowed brow that gave him a perpetually worried expression, like he was about to deliver bad news. A noisy crowd of kids had gathered around us, each vying for their turn. I already knew what was coming. I was all too familiar with disappointment.

But then, the ice cream man winced, and his expression softened to his signature friendly smile. "Actually," Mr Bassey stuttered, "it j-j-just might be yo-yo-your lucky day." My heart skipped a beat. Could it be true?

He reached behind him, digging into a hollow section of the cooler. The other kids watched with interest, curious about what he was doing. Then, he produced not one, not two, but three scoops of chocolate ice cream, each one nestled in its own cone. My eyes widened, and my mouth fell open. I couldn't believe my luck. This was the happiest day of my life.

The other kids began to ask for chocolate too, but I didn't care to see if they got any. I was too elated to pay attention. It was a moment that would stay with me forever. The ice cream man had brought a glimmer of joy to my life, like a ray of sunshine on a cloudy day.

But as I walked away licking my ice cream, my mind wandered to the empty paternal void that I felt inside. I missed my father, who only visited when my maternal grandparents allowed him to. My mother was usually away pursuing her education, and my grandfather was always travelling. That notwithstanding, my grandparents' home was a lively place in Lagos, a bustling city where the sun beat down mercilessly on its inhabitants. As soon as you stepped into the house, the

5

vibrant and dazzling colours in each room greeted you with a burst of energy. From the zesty tangerine orange to the refreshing lime green wall paints, every hue felt like a portal to a different world, beckoning you to explore and savour its unique flavour. The kitchen was my favourite place, where my grandmother cooked up a storm, creating savoury and spicy dishes that still make my mouth water at the mere recollection of their aroma. The house was always filled with the sound of music, a mix of highlife, jazz, soul, and traditional Yoruba tunes. It was a place of celebration, where every occasion was a reason to throw a party.

What I treasured most were the quiet moments spent with my grandmother. We were close, and I might even have been her favourite grandchild. My mother was the middle child, and I was her only child at the time. My aunt also lived with us and was very close to my mother. My grandmother taught me Christian values, instilling in me a strong notion of morality. She taught me to pray, and we recited the Lord's Prayer every morning. The first line, which goes "Our Father, who art in heaven", resonated with me, gave me an embrace of comfort, and always put my young mind at ease. More than just a recital, it was a reminder that even though my earthly father was absent, a higher power was still there for me. Grandma also taught me a night-time prayer she called the Black Paternoster. It goes as follows:

> Matthew, Mark, Luke, and John
> Bless the bed that I lie on
> Four angels around my bed
> Keeping watch over my head
> One to watch and one to pray
> And two to bear my soul away
> Matthew, Mark, Luke, and John

6

Bless the bed that I lie on
Amen

This prayer felt like a cuddly hug of reassuring safety from guardian angels, yet it created a concern of being swept away into eternal nothingness while I slept.

At least my soul would be at ease, I thought. Ever the optimist, I knew I had too much to live for, so faith woke me up every morning. Of course, just like any other child, I had curiosities about my environment, culture, and most especially, my Christian faith. I would ask adults, especially my grandma, questions like were Matthew, Mark, Luke, and John angels or Jesus's disciples, or maybe both? Does the garden of Eden still exist and does the Adam and Eve story contradict science? What about the dinosaurs? If the world would be destroyed in the end according to Revelations, does it mean that before the biblical creation story, "the earth being void, dark, and without form" and all, that the voidness was a result of a destroyed civilisation before the world as we know it? If Jesus said we only need to have faith as small as a mustard seed, why would he accuse a disciple, saying "O ye of little faith?" Yes, I was the annoyingly inquisitive kid that had most adults rolling their eyes and ignoring me due to my deep desire for logical explanations. My grandma did indulge my curiosity, and helped me to hone my understanding of spirituality rather than fall prey to religious dogmatism. So according to her, faith was knowingly summoning the non-existent into existence. Some, she said, practised this unintentionally, but she wanted me to always be intentional in my application of faith.

"Darling, your faith is like a seesaw," she once told me. "We always sway between faithlessness and faithfulness. Never linger on the side of the faithless for too long, always lean into the faithful. That's how you measure your faith."

7

Beyond my burgeoning awareness of faith and spirituality, I became very aware of my family dynamics, and the idea of not living with my father was very strange to me.

I remember walking to school with my mother when I was just a seven-year-old boy. It was a special day because she was usually away studying to become a teacher. But on this day, she had taken time off to walk me to school. I held her hand tightly, feeling safe and secure beside her.

As we walked down the dirt path, I looked up at my mother, the sun shining brightly behind her. "Mummy, when can I see my dad?" I asked. I had only seen him a few times in my life, and I didn't really know him at all.

My mother's smile faltered a bit, and she looked down at me with a sad expression. "Akándé mí, soon," she replied softly. "But for now, it's just you, me, Aunty Mimi, and your grandparents. You have a lot of people who love you very much."

I frowned, not entirely satisfied with her answer. "But why can't we all be together like my friends and their families?" I asked, kicking at a stray rock on the path.

My mother sighed and crouched down to my level, taking my face in her hands. "Life is complicated, Akándé mí," she explained. "Your father and I are not married, and we have followed different paths. But that doesn't mean we don't love you, and it doesn't mean you're any less important to us."

I nodded, still not entirely sure I understood. "Okay," I said quietly, and we continued walking in silence for a few moments.

As we neared the school gates, my mother embraced me in a tight hug. "Be good, my dear. I'll come to pick you up later," she expressed, her eyes overflowing with love. Though she never explicitly said it, her actions left no doubt of her affection for me.

I clung on to her, reluctant to let go, and felt a surge of sadness as she eventually pulled away. As I watched her walk away, I couldn't help but yearn for the love and affection that other children seemed to receive in their nuclear families with a mother, father, and siblings. That day, I sat in class, unable to concentrate on the lessons being taught. My mind kept wandering to my absent father and the questions that were left unanswered. It was hard not knowing when I would see my dad, but I knew that my mother and grandparents loved me, and that was enough for now.

But as the day drew towards the halfway point of the school day for lunch and playtime, my mind would temporarily forget about those worries. As I step onto the playground of my childhood memories, the air is filled with the sound of laughter, screams, and playful banter. It's break time, and the other kids are running around, jumping, and playing their favourite games. For me, this was a time to escape from the classroom, a chance to let my imagination run wild and learn valuable lessons that would stay with me for life.

As I reflect on those years, I realise that playground games were more than just a pastime. They were allegories that contributed to my preparedness for life. Take Simon Says, for example. The game taught me the importance of compliance with instructions. The strict adherence to the rules of the game instilled in me an ethos of discipline that would prove useful in later years.

Hide and seek was another game that contributed to my life skills. The art of discretion and using clues to my advantage became a valuable ability, both on the playground and in life. Similarly, musical chairs taught me about the importance of quick timing and responsiveness. It was a game that demanded focus, and the ability to think and act fast.

The unpredictable nature of Duck, Duck, Goose taught me about the importance of preparedness. In life, we never know what's around the corner, and being prepared for something as mundane as a tap on the shoulder could be the difference between life and death.

But it was tug of war that left the biggest impression on me. It was a game that demanded much more than just physical strength. It taught me the value of holding on, attentiveness, power, and teamwork, all life skills that are still with me today.

Through tug of war, I learned that a strong stance was a posture of being ready for the unexpected, which could lead to a triumphant win or an embarrassing loss. The blistering grip on the rope taught me the belief in the process of holding on, never letting go, and staying in the game. Focus was also crucial, tunnel vision, disregarding all distractions to stay in the moment. Beyond physical strength is power in the form of mental fortitude, and power is the application of knowledge to overcome all kinds of adversity. And finally, cooperation and teamwork, making sure there is oneness in mind, body, and spirit, even when it's just you.

Tug of war was a reflection of life, with its many struggles and challenges. As I think back to my walks back from the playground to the classroom – a trip I made very many times – I can't help but smile at the memories. Yet, as I reflect on my life's story, a deep sadness clutches me, knowing that some of the loved ones pertinent to my journey, would have their own lives cut short too soon.

Chapter 2

Long before I was born, the origins of my family's story began in the British colonies of Nigeria, where my maternal grandparents married in the 1950s. They soon moved to London, in the United Kingdom, bringing their first child, Ìyábò, with them to start a new life. The move was a significant change, going from the tropical heat of Nigeria to the erratic four seasons of the northern hemisphere. The father was a practising lawyer, and the mother a teacher. Despite living in the UK for some time, the mother maintained her proficiency in the Yoruba language, while slowly acquiring a hybrid accent with hints of British mannerisms.

Adébísí, and her twin brother, Adébódé, who were endearingly referred to as Bísí and Bódé, were born in London and, by virtue of the UK being their birthplace, had a claim to British citizenship. All three children went to school and settled into life in the UK. However, the call of new beginnings in Africa, with the promise of educated Africans returning to their homeland to rebuild after colonial rule, became increasingly enticing. So, the family decided to return to Nigeria in the early 1960s.

Whilst they faced challenges upon their return, such as corruption, mismanagement, and the imperialistic post-traumatic stress disorder affecting an entire nation, the parents found work, a home, and support to raise their children. A few years after returning to Nigeria, the mother gave birth to her third daughter, Abídèmí, or Mimi, who had a complicated birth and needed immediate surgery to repair a hole in her heart. The surgery left her with a bumpy scar in the centre of her chest.

Regrettably, the parents' marriage wasn't perfect, and they were estranged for years. This estrangement was as a result of the tragic death of Bódé, the boy twin. His loss loomed over the family like a dark cloud. The circumstances surrounding his death were shrouded in mystery, and no one knew exactly what had happened. One day after coming back home from a game of football, he complained of a tummy ache, then went to sleep but never woke up. The autopsy identified that his food must've been tainted. He was poisoned.

The father was always looking for ways to assert his dominance, especially when it came to the women in his life. He was a tall, slender man with a consistent stern expression, and he walked with a slight limp. He always walked around with fashionable walking sticks, to aid the stiffness in his knees that were inopportunely riddled with arthritis. He blamed his wife for the tragedy. He believed that her neglect led to Bódé's untimely demise, and he kicked her out of the house in a fit of rage. From then on, he took in a series of mistresses, each vying to bear him a son to replace the one he had lost.

The wife, on the other hand, was a tiny woman, barely five foot tall, a no-nonsense lady that always had a pep in her step. She was able to show an extreme spectrum of emotions ranging from love to anger and everything in between. She embodied the true qualities of nurturer and protector of her family. Of course, she was heartbroken by the death of her son, and there was absolutely no way she would have harmed her own, intentionally or otherwise. Despite her estrangement from her

12

husband, she found a way to live nearby to keep a keen watchful eye on her daughters, without his knowledge.

All three sisters walked on eggshells in their own home, and their father barely showed them any love. Bísí, now the middle child, was a quiet and shy girl who shared her father's height but none of his anger. She had a slim frame and a high-pitched voice, and she rarely spoke unless spoken to. Her younger sister, Mimi, was the opposite. She was carefree, loved to eat, and had an average build, plus she had a unique laugh that could be heard from a mile away. Bísí used to caution her little sister to be careful not to take food from strangers, to avoid the same demise as their brother.

The eldest sister, Ìyábò, was the spitting image of her father, with a chiselled face and her mother's fiery temper. One day, Ìyábò got into a physical altercation with one of her father's mistresses. The same mistress who had been rumoured to have killed Bódé. The argument began indoors but quickly escalated outside, so Bísí and Mimi rushed to get their mother, who lived just a few streets away, to come intervene.

Their mother arrived at the scene and quickly took matters into her own hands.

"You ought to be ashamed picking on a girl half your age," she said to the mistress in a threatening tone. "Now let's make it a fair fight!"

Despite her small, unassuming stature, she beat the mistress mercilessly, dragging her by her hair and giving her a haematoma. The police eventually arrived and arrested both women, but the father only bailed his wife out of jail. The altercation and its aftermath ended up on the local evening news by the next day.

From then on, the father promised to put his philandering days behind him and end his debaucherous cycle of mistresses.

Of course, by this time the father had fathered multiple other daughters outside of Ìyábò, Bísí and Mimi through his escapades with other women. Despite this, his wife still agreed to move back in, for the sake of her daughters, of course, but only under the condition that she and her husband slept in separate bedrooms. He obliged.

Irrespective of the turmoil in the family, Bísí always reminded herself that there was something valuable to learn from every situation. The tragedy of Bódé's death and the subsequent family drama taught her that forgiveness, as exemplified by her mother, was key to moving forward, and that love could triumph over even the darkest of circumstances. They were a group of flawed and imperfect individuals, but the family's shared love and bonds kept them together, no matter what.

As they mended their way back through years of being a broken family, Ìyábò still wasn't happy, and it was evident that she had a lot on her mind. She would sneak out every night, swearing her little sisters to secrecy, and wouldn't tell anyone where she was going. Ìyábò's adolescent rebellion manifested in more ways than just going to parties, having a boyfriend, drinking alcohol, and dressing provocatively; those were merely the visible signs of much deeper and more complex feelings of unhappiness. Her parents were worried, and even when they found out about her antics, there was little they could do to reconnect with her.

A few months went by, and just a month after her nineteenth birthday, Ìyábò got pregnant. It was a shock to the entire family, especially her parents. They had no idea who the father was or where he came from. They were furious at first, but finally warmed up to the boyfriend when they came to know him. He was an honourable military man, who sought to do the right thing by stepping up and seeking permission from Ìyábò's parents, asking for her hand in marriage, to which they agreed. They had a beautiful wedding ceremony, and soon after, they had their own home and their first child.

Bísí, on the other hand, had plans to travel back to the United Kingdom for further education. She had a best friend called Lábàké, who was also making plans of her own to travel to the UK, so they intended to keep each other company abroad. Being born there, Bísí had all the necessary documents to guarantee her easy re-entry. Or at least that's what she thought. But when it came time to seek out those documents, they were nowhere to be found. Her birth certificate, medical records, pictures of her as a child in London, and other relevant papers, all gone. Her father scolded her for her carelessness, and Lábàké went to the United Kingdom without Bísí. They stayed in touch... for a time.

— ∞ —

Years went by, and Bísí became very blasé. She didn't work or go to school, which irritated her father, and he in turn blamed his wife for encouraging Bísí's laziness.

"Why can't you be more like your older sister?" he would always ask Bísí.

Ìyábò was married, was still able to maintain a civil service job, and had now birthed four children by her mid-twenties. That may have been a yardstick for excellence in the eyes of her father, but that path wasn't one Bísí found particularly inspiring. Her father recognised her love for books in addition to her innate talent for expression, urging her to pursue a career as a paralegal at his law chambers. Bísí agreed, though she harboured misgivings about the confrontational nature of the legal profession. In this new role, Bísí found herself immersed in a variety of tasks, including attending court hearings with her father, organising case files, drafting legal documents, conducting research, and tending to administrative duties. Along the way, she struck up a close friendship with her father's secretary, who became a trusted ally in the often-challenging world of law. While Bísí's older sister had chosen a more conventional path, Bísí was determined to forge her own way and make her mark on the world.

Being attractive – in her early twenties, tall, fresh faced, with brown skin and an obvious timidity about her – Bísí was no stranger to being catcalled on the street, and she faced this on a daily basis while outdoors running errands. Her mother had always taught her how to behave in such circumstances, stating to her several times, "If you feel uncomfortable or unsafe, find a way to remove yourself from the situation as quickly as possible."

As the day wore on one precious afternoon, and the last of her father's errands were coming to an end, there remained one final task: some legal research at the nearby barrister's chambers. This lawyer, named Mr Jímọ̀h, had made appearances at her father's office and even visited their home a few times, making him a familiar face. She met with him at his chambers, which was just two streets away from where she worked. As she completed the task at hand, she engaged in pleasantries and small talk with the middle-aged man, dropping off some files before heading towards the door. Unbeknownst to her, the barrister had ulterior motives. Just as she was about to leave, he seized her hand, looking at her with a suggestive glint in his eye, and uttered, "I'd like to get to know you better."

To which she said nothing, snatched her arm back, and walked away, as fast as she could. Despite her not entertaining his advances, and him being old enough to be her father, there was something about the man she couldn't resist.

Bísí would continue to work as a paralegal for a few more years, and her father would go on a lot of work-related trips. Accra, Johannesburg, Dakar, Hamburg – he was always on the move. The father also maintained a colourful collection of fridge magnets, always bringing one back from each trip. On one trip, he took Mimi along with him to London. Bísí wrote a letter to Lábàké, whom she had missed, and gave it to Mimi to hand-deliver it to her. Lábàké had been hard to reach by all the other methods that Bísí tried. Her father would locate Lábàké's last known address using his connections. Bísí and the secretary would take care of things at the office while her father was away.

During the father's visit to London, once he had completed all his work obligations, he decided to give Mimi a proper tour of the city, since it was her first time abroad. They visited various museums, the iconic Big Ben, the vibrant West End, and a host of top-notch restaurants. Their final destination was Lábàké's residence, where her father and Mimi surprised her with their unexpected arrival. As Lábàké opened the door, the father and Mimi were overjoyed to see her, but the look of fear and guilt that flickered in her eyes did not go unnoticed. It was the type of guilt that led to shame. The type of shame that led to a confession. Lábàké's shocking confession revealed that she had stolen Bísí's "lost" documents, which would have made her re-entry into England easier. In a twisted turn of events, she had assumed Bísí's identity and betrayed her trust. The whole time Bísí and Lábàké were planning their further education overseas as friends, Lábàké had been plotting to steal her best friend's identity. Mimi's fists balled up in anger at this revelation, and the father had to intervene to physically restrain

17

her from harming Lábàké. The father, in a calm yet firm tone, asked Lábàké to return all the stolen documents immediately, and to everyone's relief, she complied. When he and Mimi went to the police station to report the theft, they later learned that Lábàké had fled her residence before the authorities could apprehend her. No arrests were made, as she had absconded, never to be seen again.

As she listened to Mimi recounting the events of London after her return to Lagos, a searing ache of regret struck Bísí. How could she have been so gullible and naive? Trust was a precious commodity, and it was rare for Bísí to trust anyone afterwards, most especially those with a penchant for being dodgy. Nevertheless, this experience taught her a valuable lesson in caution and watchfulness. Undeterred, she persevered in her work at the law chambers, fuelled by a newfound ambition to pass the bar exam and become a lawyer. That is, until she hit a roadblock…

— ∞ —

"Who is the father?" he barked at her, his eyes burning into her like hot coals. "Are you deaf? I said who is the father? Don't make me come over there and slap the truth out of your mouth!"

"It's… it's Barrister Jímọh," Bísí said nervously, with a cloak of embarrassment around her too thin to keep her from shivering. Her father was so enraged, he reverberated with anger, his tone cutting through the air like a blade. He couldn't stand the sight of Bísí any longer.

"If you seek sanctuary, go to Barrister Jímọh's home and stay with his wife and children. You are no daughter of mine!" Her father's rage only intensified, and he banished her from his home, disowning her on the spot. With no chance to gather her belongings, Bísí was left with nothing but the clothes on her back. As someone who had experienced being kicked out of that same house before, her mother consoled her and offered her a scintilla of hope. She whispered in her ear as she slyly put some money in her daughter's hand on the way out, "Go to Ìyábò's place. You'll be safe there."

Bísí's world turned upside down the day everyone else found out she was pregnant. The harsh reality of being impregnated by her father's work colleague put her in a risky situation, as she struggled to come to terms with the possibility of being labelled a homewrecker and facing the scorn of her family and community. Aside from the unsettling pattern of the father's daughters getting pregnant out of wedlock, this circumstance was particularly troubling as Bísí was carrying the child of a man who was already married with a family of his own. The father couldn't bear the shame and taboo of it all, and even took partial responsibility for possibly being the reason their paths crossed in the first place. He was utterly betrayed by Barrister Jímòh. Similarly, just like his daughter, he couldn't bear the sight of him either.

Meanwhile, Mr Jímòh had to deal with the consequences of his actions in his own home. His wife and children were left reeling from the revelation of his infidelity. He managed to keep his family together despite the naysayers. Although he still wanted to be there for Bísí and the unborn child, Bísí's father shut him out completely. Mr Jímòh's pleas were met with the utmost disdain, most especially when he suggested taking Bísí as a second wife. Obviously, any talk of bigamy was heresy to Bísí's parents.

Bísí was left in distress after having to bid farewell to her paralegal position at her father's legal firm, without any alternate job opportunities or prospects of income. The enormity of her new reality left her struggling to reconcile with it. Amidst her struggles, she found safety in the comforting embrace of her loving sister Ìyábò, who welcomed her with open arms, along with her military husband and their four little kids. To further bolster her spirits, Bísí's mother and Mimi frequently offered their unwavering support through regular visits.

As the months passed, Bísí's dreams of becoming a lawyer and pursuing her education in the UK slowly faded into the distance, while her belly grew larger with each passing day. Yet, despite the setbacks, Bísí found solace in being a beloved and fun aunt to Ìyábò's kids. In the company of the little ones, the idea of motherhood became more alluring to her. She understood that living with her sister was only a temporary solution, so she made sure to express her gratitude by cooking, cleaning, and taking care of her nephews and nieces to the best of her ability. One morning, while she was out shopping for maternity outfits on her own, a mere three weeks before her due date, she had a brief moment of incontinence in the middle of a shop. After the unexpected wetness in her undergarments, which was now leaking, she recoiled in embarrassment, assuming she had lost control of her bladder. She actually thought it was a random third trimester symptom and continued with her shopping, hoping no one had noticed. She got everything she needed from the shop and casually headed back home to her sister's place. It was not until she recounted the incident to her sister Ìyábò, hours later, that she came to the shocking realisation that her water had broken. Frantic, Ìyábò took Bísí to the hospital that same evening, chiding Bísí as to why she didn't speak sooner and over the potential risk to the baby. By the time Bísí got a hospital bed, it was almost midnight. Her baby boy was born shortly thereafter without any complications. It was 1:15 am on a Friday.

$$- \infty -$$

Within weeks, word of my birth had gotten around to the rest of the family.

My arrival brought about reconciliation between my mother and grandfather. However, it wasn't until three months after my birth, that he welcomed us back to his home. Living in his house, I would grow to love my grandpa and grandma, without knowing any of the events that had transpired before my birth. As an infant, I existed in a state of bliss and obliviousness, fully unaware of my own existence or the world around me. But as I matured, I gradually gained awareness and consciousness, recognising the fickle hand of fate that had brought me into being. No choice or agency of my own, I was simply the product of my parents' actions – deliberate or not. It's a haunting realisation, one that can leave any child in a lingering state of guilt or shame, especially if the world into which one is born is one of rejection, chaos, or strife. Yet I chose to cling to my innocence, ridding myself of any blame, while learning to refuse being tainted by the heavy weight of stigma attached to my conception, and embracing my family's affection.

Chapter 3

As I celebrated my seventh birthday, my father's family remained unknown to me. In contrast, my maternal family was a handful, to say the least. Luckily, I forged a close bond with Aunty Ìyábò's children, who wholeheartedly embraced me as their cousin and treated me like a beloved sibling. I found myself shuffling between my grandparents' home and Aunty Ìyábò's farm, which was home to a myriad of livestock and crops. Every morning, my cousins would handpick fresh ingredients for breakfast, creating meals that were both delicious and nourishing. One of my fondest memories was climbing guava trees during a rousing game of hide and seek, where a couple of us would remain hidden for hours, munching on fruit while the others searched for us in vain. We also took care of the farm animals, feeding the chickens, collecting freshly laid eggs, bathing the dogs, and clipping the wool of the sheep. We tended to the crops, watering and harvesting them with great care. Through it all, we developed a deep connection to nature that was both humbling and awe-inspiring. The home was disciplined yet fun, a testament to the strict yet kind influence of their military-minded father.

As a young boy, I discovered an ability that usually left me feeling confused and scared. It was the ability to dream every time I went to sleep. Every night, my dreams were vivid, ranging from the comical to the bizarre, but I would tend to forget about the dreams not long after waking up. Some nights, I would dream of events that played out like déjà vu in my waking hours days later. But one night while I was at Aunty Ìyábò's farmstead, I had a dream that stood out from the rest – a mind-boggling premonition of a family member's demise. Despite its troubling intensity, the dream faded from my memory as quickly as it had come, leaving me with an uneasy feeling I couldn't shake.

Aunty Ìyábò was always one to keep her home in perfect order, but it was the madness of her father's affairs that kept her up at night. The constant barrage of strange women and their children at my grandparents' front door, seeking validation and legitimacy despite being jilted by Grandpa, was just the tip of the iceberg. A shocking family secret came to light, revealing that someone Aunty Ìyábò had grown up to know as her amiable second cousin was, in fact, her half-sister through incest. Grandma had had no idea either, which meant she'd married her husband without knowing he already had a secret love child. This love child was the result of a teenage affair between Grandpa and his cousin, the mother – who had been sworn to secrecy, keeping the child's true parentage hidden. The closeness between Aunty Ìyábò and her once-cousin-now-half-sister obviously became sour. The revelation sent shockwaves through the family, leaving everyone bewildered except for Grandpa. It didn't help matters that other women and their children began to emerge, claiming to be Grandpa's offspring, some with reasonable evidence to back up their claims while others were mere opportunists, claiming to have birthed his much sought-after male child. Those claims of male children were unfortunately fictitious. Old mistresses also crawled out of the woodwork, seeking to force their way back into Grandpa's life and take up residence in his house with their little ones permanently. It was a civil war, and Aunty Ìyábò was more than ready to fight alongside Grandma. But as for me, a child at the time, if only I'd had the audacity to speak to Aunty Ìyábò, I would have reminded her that it wasn't her fight. My mother, a quiet pacifist, wanted no part of the in-fighting and always warned Aunty Mimi to stay out of it. Gossip and rumours gradually took form, suggesting that Grandpa, who had now passed his seventies, had enlisted the expertise of a separate legal practitioner to prepare his final will and testament. One thing you quickly learn about living in the city of Lagos is that money talks, and anyone could bribe their way into accessing classified materials such as the final will and testament of any individual. And soon enough, with the revelation of his hidden wealth and assets, the dispute over his estate began, with certain family members jostling to claim their share of my grandfather's estate while he still breathed. At the time, I had no inkling of my grandfather's wealth, but it soon became apparent that he owned a vast number of properties, assets, bonds, and shares in both local and foreign conglomerates, most of which Grandma was completely unaware of.

Months later, as the squabble for my grandfather's assets escalated into a violent free-for-all, it became clear that an intervention of some sort was the necessary path to follow. More of Grandpa's children emerged from the shadows, clawing for their share of their inheritance. In a bid to quell the disarray, Grandpa called for a family meeting, but it only served to stir up more trouble. My mother, Aunty Ìyábò, Aunty Mimi, and eight other siblings were to be gathered in a room, alongside their mothers, each vying for a place in the family hierarchy.

The location Grandpa chose for this family meeting had to be on neutral territory, definitely not his home. It ended up being a large hotel conference room, fully air-conditioned, with long rows of chairs arranged in straight lines and a large stage set up at the front of the room. The walls were painted a bland shade of off-white, and the carpet underfoot was a dull grey. As the children Grandpa had sired began to arrive, an unmistakable undertone of tension settled over the room. Some of them arrived alone, while others came with their mothers or other family members. There were murmurs of recognition as some of the sisters finally saw each other face to face for the very first time, their resemblance to each other undeniable. But as the meeting began, it quickly became clear that the overriding concerns for many of the participants in the room were acceptance, inheritance, and the distribution of his assets. Some of the sisters were clearly more interested in the financial benefits of their father's legacy than in forging a relationship with each other.

The tension in the room continued to grow as the meeting wore on, with accusations and recriminations flying back and forth. The air grew thick with the scent of anger and resentment, as sisters who had never met before found themselves embroiled in unfounded arguments. Grandpa's suggestion for his children to introduce themselves by age only added fuel to the fire. As tempers flared and voices grew louder, Aunty Ìyábò and her once-cousin-now-half-sister stood up at the same time, both insisting on being called "first born".

What followed was a brawl of epic proportions – punches were thrown, wigs were snatched, and screams echoed through the air. The dust settled and injuries were tended to, but regrettably, that family meeting yielded no true benefits. Tragically, just less than twenty-four hours after that family meeting, Aunty Ìyábò began to feel gravely ill, her condition mysterious and terrifying.

The sickness that had befallen Aunty Ìyábò was something that felt almost otherworldly, as if it were the result of a twisted fetish or some sort of dark magic. In a country like Nigeria, where the ancient beliefs of idol worship and supernatural charms held sway long before the advent of Christianity, such things were not unheard of. After that tumultuous family meeting, rumours began to circulate that someone had placed a curse upon her, causing her health to rapidly decline. Despite numerous medical and spiritual interventions, nothing seemed to work. She eventually passed away just a month later. It wasn't until I received news of her death that I got the epiphany that what I had experienced was a déjà rêvé – a fully materialised premonition of sorts. I couldn't shake the feeling that I had seen this all before – in a dream that I had long forgotten but now haunted me with the knowledge that I could have done something to stop it. In my dream, it was my dear Aunty Ìyábò that I had seen die, and the reality that played out before me now was something I could have never imagined.

The death of Aunty Ìyábò left my family in shambles. My grandma's sobs filled the air with despair, as she blamed my baffled grandpa for the loss. In a bid to cope with her grief, Aunty Mimi chose a peculiar approach. Now in her late teens, she found solace in imitating Ìyábò's old teenage antics, including attending parties, dating a man named Tajúdéẹn – or Uncle Taj, as I referred to him – consuming alcohol, and dressing provocatively, among other things. Perhaps Aunty Mimi felt a connection with Aunty Ìyábò's adolescent rebellious streak. Maybe by adopting some of her sister's former attitudes, values, and behaviours, she'd found a way to feel closer to her sister in order to cope with the loss. It's also probable that Aunty Mimi's adoption of Aunty Ìyábò's old behaviour was a means of establishing her own identity and asserting her independence, much like Aunty Ìyábò at the same age. By emulating her sister's former conduct, Aunty Mimi was probably attempting to carve out her unique identity in order to break free from the fetters of her grief.

For a brief time, my mother coped with her grief by imposing a solemn vow of silence upon herself towards everyone else, apart from me. As I observed Aunty Ìyábò's children lost in their own confusion and inconsolable pain, I couldn't shake off the burning guilt that consumed me. It prevented me from being the comfort they desperately needed and instead made me unconsciously distance myself from them. Amidst the mourning, I held on to a secret that had been haunting me – a dream that I had never shared with anyone. But when I finally mustered the courage to confide in my mother, she embraced me and lit a spark of hope. She urged me to keep a dream journal, to record every detail of my dreams, especially if they involved our family or hinted at any impending danger.

"Write down as many of your dreams as you possibly can, Akándé mí," my grieving mother said to me.

Soon enough, my mother gifted me several notepads. The soft leather covers felt supple and warm in my hands. Each was a rich chocolate brown, and I could smell the faint scent of leather mixed with the sweet aroma of freshly printed paper. Running my fingers over the smooth surface, I opened each book to reveal pristine white pages, waiting to be filled with my delightful or dreadful dreams and vanishing visions. As I flipped through the rustling pages, the faint lines on each page caught my attention – perfectly spaced for writing. It had about four hundred pages, enough to contain a year's worth of dreams if I woke up every day with one. I could picture myself waking up from a dream in the early hours of the morning and reaching for my dream journal, my pen scratching across the page as I scribbled down every detail before it faded from memory.

My mother's thoughtful gift was more than just a simple journal; it meant I could give much-needed warnings from my dreams without forgetting them. I put one of the dream journals on my bedside table, so I could turn to it whenever I woke up with another dream. With a burst of determination, thrust into the waking world after every new dream, I began to write them down – from the silly ones to the ones that felt more significantly serious. Some of my journalled dreams included:

March 6th 6:05 am: Being chased by a mysterious figure.

March 7th 6:51 am: Chasing after the same mysterious figure.

March 11th 5:47 am: Finding myself in a classroom unprepared for an exam.

March 15th 6:01 am: Winning a lottery jackpot and deciding how to spend the money.

March 16th 4:50 am: Being lost in a labyrinthine maze.

March 17th 6:03 am: Swimming with dolphins in a crystal-clear ocean.

March 22nd 7:09 am: Conducting a symphony orchestra in front of a large audience.

March 25th 7:01 am: Travelling through time and witnessing historical events.

March 31st 6:57 am: Participating in a thrilling car race.

April 1st 6:23 am: Being able to control the weather.

April 4th 5:48 am: Visiting an alien planet and encountering extra-terrestrial beings.

April 7th 6:24 am: Becoming invisible and exploring places undetected.

April 11th 7:03 am: Being able to breathe underwater and exploring an enchanting underwater world.

April 14th 5:59 am: Lost in a magical forest filled with talking animals and mythical creatures.

April 17th 6:52 am: On a thrilling roller coaster ride that twists and turns through mountains made out of ice cream.

April 25th 6:44 am: Finding myself in a haunted house and uncovering its secrets.

April 27th 6:08 am: Getting kidnapped and plotting my escape.

April 29th 6:41 am: Becoming a detective and solving a complex crime.

May 2nd 6:36 am: Skateboarding on a rainbow with my cousins.

Amidst the mystifying concoction of dreams that filled my mind, hope remained: that this very journal, in all its many pages, could serve as a conduit for clarity, untangling the intricate threads of my thoughts, and offering solace for the weighty burden of my silence concerning Aunty Ìyábò.

Months passed after Aunty Ìyábò's burial, and just when the family was starting to heal, I had another dream. This time, the person in danger was my own mother. The dream was so vivid, I could feel the terror pulsing through me. As soon as I woke up, I scrambled to jot down every single detail in my dream journal. When I told my mum about it, she tried to reassure me that everything would be fine, but I could see the worry in her eyes.

Days went by, filled with prayers, fasting, and every intervention possible to protect my mother from harm. And then, just a week later, I had another dream. This one felt like a continuation of the previous one. In it, I found myself sitting at a table in a restaurant, waiting for my mother. She appeared, looking dishevelled and terrified, as if she had been held captive for months. In spite of her tattered appearance in the dream, I was overjoyed to see her. As I asked her what she wanted to eat, she stared at me with intense eyes that seemed to say so much yet revealed nothing. The waiter brought over a platter of food, and my mother devoured everything in sight, without saying a word. Watching her eat brought me an indescribable feeling of relief and happiness, even as she continued to stare at me with a look that was hard to read.

When I woke up, I immediately wrote down every single detail and showed my dream journal to my mother. It was then that we both knew that our prayers had been answered, and my mother was safe. Regardless of the lingering fear, there was also a feeling of optimism that everything would be okay.

Even with the shroud of grief that had enveloped our family, a ray of hope shone like the sun rising from the east. My mother's radiant smile had returned, and she had found happiness in the arms of a single dad with a young son. She was also eagerly awaiting a new baby. Before long, I found myself part of a small family unit consisting of my mother, stepfather, stepbrother Wálé, and a baby half-brother, Ẹnítàn, all living together in a place of our own, separate from my grandparents' home. Her new family embraced me with open arms, and I spent most weekends with them, feeling accepted and loved. In this period, I also had the opportunity to get to know my father, Mr Jímọ̀h, a little better. It felt as though a fresh chapter had unfurled in my life, one that was filled with warmth, love, and the promise of stability in my formative years.

Chapter 4

As a child, the local ice cream man seemed more familiar to me than my own father, who was, for all intents and purposes, a stranger in my life. Be that as it may, not long after my eighth birthday, he began to visit me at my grandparents' home more frequently and expressed his desire to introduce me to his family. He was persistent, despite the years it took to overcome the hurdle of my grandparents' disapproval towards him. My grandma eventually became more accepting of his visits and allowed him to take me out shopping, to parks, and to restaurants. He even arranged for my Anglican baptism in his church. Despite the minimal risk inherent in spending time with my own father, my grandma remained protective and cautious. She wanted my father's wife to come over to their house and embrace me as her own child, but she never did. Maybe my father never conveyed the message to her. Nonetheless, he eventually took me to his house for short visits, where I only met a few of my older siblings and his wife, who surprisingly showed me kindness.

Though my father and grandmother rarely saw eye to eye on matters concerning me, their intentions were rooted in my best interest. My non-confrontational mother often left Grandma to handle discussions about my upbringing with my father. I do believe, however, that both sides agreeing to send me to boarding school was a wise choice, and I wholeheartedly complied. Along with the rigorous academic standards, I struggled with being homesick, constant bullying, and the appalling living conditions of the all-boys school. As I was a boarding student, family visits were limited to the last Sunday of each month, yet my mother managed to send me care packages filled with biscuits, milk, cereal, and noodles through some day students almost every week. My father would also occasionally stop by on his way home from work, and we would chat in his car about my studies and school life.

Boarding school instilled discipline in me early on, especially with the whirring sound of the siren that could shatter the tranquil silence of the night, echoing through the dormitory walls and vibrating every bone in my body, dragging me out of my warm bed at the ungodly hour of 5:30 am every weekday. I could even have my dreams interrupted, but I always made sure to write whatever I remembered in my dream journal, as soon as I was awoken. Shower time became a game of chance, where the feeble water pressure could barely reach the second floor, forcing me to take a gamble on such occasions by fetching a bucket of water from a tap located hundreds of metres away. The queue for the borehole tap was usually long and daunting – the mere thought of the wait would be enough to discourage me from attempting to take a shower on such days. The dining hall's mediocre food still managed to leave me salivating, despite the cruelly long waiting periods between meals. In my quest for academic excellence, I knew that maintaining good grades was a must, as it was my ticket to becoming a medical doctor, accountant, engineer, or whatever job paid the bills. Boarding school not only helped me to cultivate multiple learning patterns and discipline, but also fostered my toughness. Yet, amidst all of this, political turmoil raged on, with a dictator's demise allegedly caused by a poisoned apple, debates on transitioning from military to democratic rule, poverty, and the paranoia of insecurity that permeated even the walls of a secondary school. This is what living in Nigeria felt like in the late 1990s.

— ∞ —

As the sun began to set on the day of an annually held alumni reunion, the air was filled with an uncomfortable tension. The sound of revving engines and screeching tyres echoed through the busy campus as the wealthy elites arrived in their flashy sports cars and convertibles. Those alumni loved to show off. I had just left the dining hall, clutching a styrofoam container of hot custard and bean cakes, when chaos erupted. Panicked screams and shouts shattered the stillness of the evening, and the sound of heavy footsteps pounding the ground filled my ears. Suddenly, a gang of at least a dozen masked bandits burst through the gates, wielding weapons and threatening everyone in their path.

As I watched from the second-floor balcony, I could see the glint of their guns in the moonlight as they menaced the helpless students below. It was clear that they had come for the cars – the prized possessions of the wealthy alumni. I tried to make my way back to my dormitory, but then the electricity went out – I could barely see. The frightened crowd pushed and shoved against me, forcing me to stumble. That's when I heard the deafening sound of rattling gunfire, and bullets whizzing past me with frightening speed. Suddenly, I felt a searing pain in my torso and collapsed to the ground, clutching at my shirt in terror. The warm liquid that soaked through my fingers felt thick and sticky. I was crying at this point, screaming "Somebody, help me!" and was certain that I was going to die.

Through the haze of pain and fear, I heard a familiar voice calling my name. It was my friend, who had pulled me out of the way of the stampeding crowd.

"Relax, dude. You're fine, it's just custard." He smirked mockingly, looking a little too unbothered by the pandemonium.

My hot dinner had spilled all over me in the chaos. I let out a sigh, grateful for the respite, but embarrassment lingered for thinking I was soaked in blood when in fact it was just custard. Thankfully, no one was killed that night, but the memory of the gunshots and the fear they brought with them stayed with me for a long time. The armed robbers made away with nine luxury cars that night.

Experiencing gun violence as a pre-teen was a traumatic event. Even at that age, I thought about the mass shootings that occurred in American schools and how their corrupt governments continually failed to protect their institutions due to relaxed gun-control laws. Luckily, there weren't many school shootings in the United Kingdom compared to the US, but I would later discover that I still had to be careful about knife crime. At least stray stab wounds weren't a common occurrence. No country is perfect, and each has its peculiarities, and that fateful night at school was a turning point for me. I was determined to seek out an education abroad, one that was better than what my current country of residence had to offer. I didn't fully understand the intricacies of immigration laws across the world; despite this, I believed that studying in an international school would broaden my horizons, help me overcome any culture shock, and possibly remove any fears of insecurities in institutions. I needed to come up with a well-planned strategy to pursue further education abroad. Maybe someday, I could make that happen.

News of the robbery at my school spread quicker than I could have imagined. Using the payphone at the school's phone booth, I hastily contacted my grandmother, who promptly arrived in Grandpa's car, along with their driver, the very next day. The campus was in disarray as parents scurried about, packing up their children's belongings in a frenzy. Uncertain about how long the school's temporary closure would last, I made multiple trips to my dormitory to retrieve all my belongings. The first trip included my bulky mattress and backpack, which I stowed away in the boot of my grandparents' car.

I approached my grandmother and informed her, "Just one bag left, then we can go." She nodded in agreement and urged me to hurry. I turned to head back to the dormitory, and out of nowhere I caught sight of my father standing around a hundred metres away, motioning for me to come towards him.

I was perplexed, and when I approached him, I queried, "When did you get here?"

His response was brief and commanding. "Never mind that. Go get your things so we can go home."

Confused, I asked, "Home? But Grandma is already here. She's waiting for me to get my last bag so I can leave with her."

"Not to worry, son. You're coming with me," my father said in a subtle yet imposing manner. "I'll have a word with her by the time you're back with your bag." I trusted him to keep his word.

When I went back upstairs to retrieve my final bag, I searched my dorm room thoroughly to ensure that nothing of importance was left behind. Upon my return, instead of turning left towards my grandmother, who was still standing by the car, I turned right towards my father, bag in hand, ready to leave. As I slid into my father's car, my eyes met with Grandma's driver's, who was pointing at me as he caught sight of me amongst the crowd. I couldn't hear him, but I could almost read his lips. He must have said, "He's over there." My grandmother's gaze turned in the direction of his pointed finger, and I knew I was in trouble. From a distance, I could see her agitation swell, building up like a storm on the horizon. It suddenly dawned on me that my father had not said a word to my grandma.

The silence during the drive to my dad's house was disconcerting. He tried to engage me in small talk, but my responses were short and curt. The cloud of betrayal grew, and I wondered if my father had any idea of what he was doing. When we arrived, some of my siblings welcomed me with open arms, momentarily easing my disconcertment.

But within moments, a familiar car horn was blaring outside the gate. It was my grandmother, and her fury was palpable. Only upon their arrival did I realise that we were probably in a car chase the whole time. We stood frozen as she pulled up, her eyes scanning the porch. Our eyes locked, and I could sense her anger mounting. I knew what was coming.

She emerged from the car, waving her finger at my father. Her words came out like venom, stinging everyone in earshot. "Just because you have a fancy car and a house, that doesn't make you a good father! You dare disregard me and run off with him like this? What a joke you are!" Her words hit me like friendly fire. I felt the weight of her disapproval and disappointment, unable to bring myself to look at my father.

She turned to me, reaching out her hand. "Let's go." I had no choice but to comply. My grandma was my beacon of morality, and I could never object to her. I avoided eye contact with my father and grabbed my bag, holding tightly on to her hand as we headed back to her car. As we drove away, I watched my father and siblings shrink in the rear-view mirror, wondering if I would ever see them again.

Despite the fiasco at my school with my father and grandmother, the anticipation of the Easter break filled me with excitement as I looked forward to doing something fun with family. My grandma had organised a trip to the zoo with all her grandchildren, and we were eager to go. It had been ages since I last saw Aunty Ìyábò's children, but we quickly rekindled our bond as if nothing had changed. The bus she hired was enormous, and my mum and Aunty Mimi were our chaperones for the day. It felt like a grand adventure, and we were thrilled. The bus was stocked with all sorts of homemade snacks – the crunchy, deep-fried biscuit-like snack made from a dough flavoured with sugar, butter, and spices, known as chin-chin, in addition to plantain chips, sausage rolls, Scotch eggs, cakes, meat pies, bean pudding, also known as moin-moin, and an array of drinks. It was like a feast on wheels. Ironically, for someone who loved food, Aunty Mimi hardly ate, indicating that she felt nauseated the entire journey. We set off for the zoo, located just outside Lagos in the beautiful city of Ibadan. As the bus carried us on the road trip, we spotted scenic views, landmarks, iconic statues, and a number of roadside attractions on the way, all of which generated more excitement in the air. We chattered away, eager to arrive at the zoo and begin our adventure. As soon as we entered the gates, we were met with the sight of majestic lions roaring and fierce crocodiles bellowing. A quiver of unease began to creep up within me. The squawking ostriches and laughing hyenas added to the cacophony of sounds filling the air, but something about their captivity made me feel uneasy. These animals were displaced from their natural habitat, caged, and confined for our entertainment and profit, all under the guise of preservation. As

I watched them pace back and forth in their enclosures, a prickling sting of guilt and discomfort came over me. Nevertheless, we had a great day, and as we headed back, we sang songs and reminisced about the day's events.

— ∞ —

As we approached home, we were met with an unexpected turn of events. I sat all the way in the back seat of the bus, my forehead pressed against the cool glass window, watching as the cars ahead of us inched forward, bumper to bumper, the sound of honking horns and frustrated drivers filling my ears, while the smells of exhaust fumes and hot tarmac made me feel sick to my stomach. We were inopportunely stuck in a rush-hour traffic jam. Suddenly, the traffic came to a complete stop, and we sat there for what felt like an eternity until we finally reached the source of the delay – a mangled wreck of a car, its twisted metal and shattered glass scattered across the road, the pungent smell of smoke and burning rubber filling the air as flames licked at the edges of the vehicle. I became unsettled as I recognised the car model, and the sickening realisation hit me that someone I knew could be involved in that accident. We drove past the wreckage, the heat of the flames radiating through the bus window as we made our way home in silence. The plan was to drop off my cousins at their farmhouse, my mum and younger siblings at my stepdad's, and then follow Aunty Mimi and Grandma home. Once we had taken everyone else to their destinations, we arrived home. There were two visitors waiting at the door. The first was a lawyer, a familiar face who had visited Grandpa often at the house, and the other was a complete stranger, most probably a colleague of his as well. As we descended from the bus, the lawyers approached my grandmother and pulled her aside with an air of urgency. Aunty Mimi went ahead of us, retching vomit into her hands as she ran to the bathroom; she was clearly sick. Staying back with my grandmother, I turned to see the fatigue on Grandma's face twist into a mask of mournful dread. Little did I know that we were about to receive earth-shattering news. We soon learned from the lawyers that Grandpa and his driver had been in a fatal accident just hours before. As the realisation hit us, I suddenly remembered the familiar, mangled car we had driven past earlier. It was Grandpa's, and we had unknowingly witnessed the scene of the accident. It also turned out that Aunty Mimi was pregnant.

Within months, a will reading was planned at the same venue where all of Grandpa's kids had met for the very first time. The same large hotel conference room with long rows of chairs arranged in straight lines, and a large stage set up at the front. Given the recent tragedies, the mood was a lot more sombre, compared to the previous time Grandpa's daughters and former mistresses had all gathered in the same room. The same lawyers who had come to our doorstep to deliver the news to my grandmother at home would preside over the will reading. Grandma, my mother, and Aunty Mimi were also present. The will's details showed that Grandpa had been petty and vindictive in his bequests:

I, Barrister Samson Adébáyọ̀, being of sound mind and body, hereby declare my last will and testament. I possess five properties in and around Lagos, multiple bank accounts, investments in stocks and bonds, and other assets. I have a wife, who bore me three daughters, and I acknowledge the existence of my eight other illegitimate children and their mothers.

Firstly, I must address the fact that my wife, who lives in one of my properties, will have limited access to my assets. This is due to her refusal to lend me a meagre sum of £20 in the 1960s. This spiteful act of hers will not be forgotten and will have consequences.

Secondly, to my legitimate daughters, I must express my disappointment in their lack of discipline and career pursuits despite my expenses in their education. I have no desire to leave them any monetary assets, as they have not lived up to my expectations.

Thirdly, to my illegitimate children, I acknowledge their rightful status as my children and therefore, they will have an equal share of my assets to my legitimate daughters. I have equal affection for them as I do for my legitimate children.

Fourthly, I bequeath my law books in my office to any of my children or grandchildren who decide to study law. This will serve as a reminder of my legacy as a legal practitioner.

Fifthly, to the property my wife and daughter(s) reside in, I split the ownership according to rooms. Each of my children, including the illegitimate ones (whom I have now legitimatised), will have one room or boys' quarters to themselves.

Sixthly, I leave the rest of all of my finances, assets, properties, investments, stocks and bonds towards creating an arthritis foundation centre in my name. No member of my family should be involved in the inner workings of this organisation, and I leave the establishment of this charity foundation in the capable hands of my lawyers. I would also like my collection of walking sticks removed from my home, to be on display at the foundation centre.

Lastly, I caution all my beneficiaries against rejecting or opposing the contents of this will. Any such actions will render their designated assets void. I urge them to accept their inheritance without any legal action.

In conclusion, this is my final declaration of my assets and property. I leave it to my executors and beneficiaries, and I hope they will abide by my wishes. Any opposition to this will only serve to prove their unworthiness of my legacy.

— ∞ —

In the wake of my grandfather's passing, I was confronted with the realisation that his marriage to my grandmother was flawed in more ways than I could ever comprehend. As I, my grandma, and Aunty Mimi sifted through his private belongings in his bedroom, we uncovered yet more evidence of his infidelity throughout the years, locked away in the different sections of his bedroom that he had kept sacred and secret. The weight of this discovery proved a crushing burden for my grandmother, who had always been devoted to him with unwavering loyalty.

But it was the spiteful venom and petty jabs he had inscribed in his will, directed at his own children and her, that proved to be the final straw for my grandmother. Already burdened with grief and suffering, she could not bear the betrayal from the man she had loved and been faithful to for most of her life. It was not long after the reading of that will that my grandmother succumbed to a stress-induced cardiomyopathy, despite never having any history of heart disease. Yet another tragic loss that left our family reeling. My grandmother and grandfather were buried right next to each other. Their passing felt like the end of my childhood, the final curtain call on an era that would shape the rest of my life. Yet in the midst of all this heartbreak,

I found a powerful lesson in my grandmother's example of love and loyalty. I saw how her resilience and commitment had sustained her through the toughest of times, and how she had always been there for my grandfather despite his flaws. Though she is no longer with us, her legacy endures, through me and the rest of her descendants.

Act II: Adolescence

"Leaving childhood's shore,
Grief-marked boy seeks father's love,
Adolescence dawns."
- Tòbí

Chapter 5

Growing up, I was fortunate enough to have three main father figures in my life: my grandfather, my biological father, and my stepfather. Each of them played a significant role in shaping who I am today, for better and for worse.

My grandfather was a hard-working man, but he could also be emotionally distant at times. He taught me to be self-reliant, but sometimes I wished he would show more affection, and he occasionally treated me like an inconvenience, which, as a child, made me slightly insecure. Through him, I did learn about our ancient family's history, traditions, and cultural heritage, helping me cultivate a sense of belonging and identity. It is a shame that he's gone now, but thankfully, there were other men I could look up to.

My father, Mr Jímọh, was a complex and intriguing figure in my life. From my earliest memories, his face was etched in my mind, yet he was often absent due to a temporary ban on seeing me. So, his absence in my formative years was not for lack of trying. He prided himself on being both a lawyer and a farmer. I heard many stories of my father's life, and I began to understand the depth of his character. As a child from a rural village, born into a family of farmers, he was determined to receive an education, no matter the cost. He was able to manoeuvre his way around school administrators, claiming to be five years younger just to gain access into the entry-level classes. He worked tirelessly to achieve his goals, ultimately becoming a highly respected lawyer by graduating from a well-renowned university in the UK. After this, he became a naturalised British citizen, while frequently travelling between Nigeria and the UK for work.

My father was a man of many rules, and he expected his children to follow them without exception. But despite his strict demeanour, there was a fairness and integrity to his character that commanded respect. His toughness came from a place of love, a desire to see us reach our full potential and become the best versions of ourselves.

My stepfather was a journalist and a gentleman. Having a stepfather directly and involuntarily taught me how to respect and accept other people's choices. Especially my mother's decision to choose him, as I was still grappling with the conflict of my birth parents never being married. He accepted me. I accepted Wálé, his son from a different marriage, as my own brother, who himself was making an effort to accept my mother. I accepted my stepfather and my mother's discreet court wedding ceremony too.

After my grandparents passed away, I spent a lot of time oscillating between the homes of my stepfather and father when I wasn't at boarding school. While each of these father figures may have had their strengths and weaknesses, they all provided me with the love, support, and guidance that I needed to thrive. Even when they made mistakes or struggled with their own challenges, I was able to learn valuable life lessons from them and develop into a well-rounded individual. Because of them, I firmly believe that being surrounded by imperfect father figures is better than having none at all. Without these individuals in my life, I would still have unanswered questions about what it means to be a man. Their influence has given me the bedrock of stability and consistency that has helped me navigate the challenges and uncertainties of life.

— ∞ —

As I stepped into my birth father's home, I knew that I had some catching up to do. My formative years had been spent at my grandparents' home, and everything here felt unfamiliar. But my father was patient, and he guided me through this new world. He taught me how to drive, sitting beside me as I grasped the wheel, watching over me with his stern gaze, waiting to chastise any mistakes I made on the road. And of course, he was hesitant to let me drive alone, and I could always see the worry etched on his face whenever I asked to drive his car.

He showed me a different side to farming from what I had learned on Aunty Ìyábò's farmstead, which included caring for the land and its inhabitants. As we worked the soil and tended to the animals, I could feel the dirt under my fingernails, the weight of the tools in my hands, in addition to the abattoir-style treatment I had to perform on some of the farm animals, getting them ready for dinner, providing food and nourishment for our home. And through it all, my love for reading grew, nurtured by my father's encouragement. As he read his favourite novels with me, his voice rising and falling with the story's ebbs and flows, I was transported to far-off places and fantastic realms.

But above all, my father's family had a guiding motto, a mantra that he instilled in us all. It was a reminder to accept and adapt to life's challenges, and my father had printed it and hung it all over the house, from the kitchen to the bedrooms. I could see it everywhere, a constant reminder of the love that bound his family together, and the need to stay grounded as we navigated the twists and turns of life.

IN PURSUIT OF HAPPINESS
Be kind, wherever you may be.
Work diligently, enjoy life, savour each meal.
For a prolonged existence, shun alcohol and smoking.
Strive for excellence in virtuous pursuits.
Above all, cherish God, your homeland, and mankind.
May divine love shower blessings upon you all.

He ensured that his children, all my older siblings, had the best education. I saw them one after the other leave Nigeria to settle in the UK, most of them married now with their own families. The state of the country, its corruption, and limited opportunities had most people in the country fleeing – not just for the UK, but other parts of Europe, America, Australia, and Asia. It made me wonder what the results of a Nigerians-in-diaspora census would turn out to be. Definitely in the tens of millions.

While at my father's home one day, I sat in the living room, staring at the pile of textbooks on the coffee table in front of me. My heart felt heavy with the weight of the uncertainty that lay ahead of me. My father was reading the newspaper, but I knew he was aware of my presence.

"Dad, can we talk?" I asked, trying to sound casual. In my adolescence, I still found it very hard to be relaxed and informal around my father. I couldn't resist the sudden feelings of nervousness that would overwhelm me, and I always felt the need to enunciate and pick my words carefully around him.

"Sure, son, what's on your mind?" my father replied, folding the newspaper and giving me his full attention.

I hesitated for a moment, trying to put my thoughts into words. "I want to go to a university in the UK, to study computer science, or something technology-adjacent," I said finally.

My father looked at me with a mixture of surprise and pride. "That's a big step, son, but I'm proud of you for wanting to pursue your dreams."

I exhaled in relief. My father had always been supportive of my academic pursuits, but I had still been nervous about his reaction.

"The university strikes and shutdowns in Nigeria have left me feeling uncertain about my future here," I explained. "I want to study in a place where I can have a stable academic environment."

My father nodded, understanding the predicament I was in. "I understand where you're coming from, son. You should always strive for the best education possible."

But then, the doubts started to creep in. "But what about Mum's British citizenship dispute?" I asked, feeling a pang of guilt for having such privilege. "Will that make it harder for me to get a visa or travel to the UK?"

My mother's identity theft was now an open case at the British embassy in Lagos, and had resulted in a complicated dispute over her British citizenship. It was a stressful situation, one that had my mother going there several times a year, with her pleas for justice being overlooked; therefore, I worried that her circumstances would make things difficult for me as well.

My father placed a reassuring hand on my shoulder. "Don't worry, son. I will find a way to make the process much smoother for you. Everything will go according to plan."

Despite my gratitude towards my father, a feeling of ambivalence overwhelmed me as I acknowledged that not many other Nigerians had access to the same privileges I was exposed to. But I also knew full well that I had to put my own priorities first.

"Dad, I know how fortunate I am to have this privilege," I expressed, with a weighty feeling on my chest. "But I want you to know that I will never take this for granted, and I will work hard every day to maximise this opportunity and hopefully make meaningful contributions to society."

My father's pride beamed through his smile as he replied, "I know you will, son. You have a bright future ahead of you, and I'm excited to see where this journey takes you. Just remember to work hard."

"Of course, I will study very hard," I replied quickly, but his expression made me realise my response may not have been what he had hoped for.

"No, I mean actual work," my father clarified, trying to be both encouraging and logical. "You won't be eligible for student loans, so you'll need to work at least twenty hours a week to pay off your fees while you're in university. I can help you with your visa or right-of-abode travel document, but I won't be able to pay your fees as they are too expensive. I will give your siblings abroad the heads-up on your intentions too."

"I understand, Dad. Thank you," I said.

As I left the room, my heart felt lighter. Even if the road ahead would be challenging, I knew I had my father's support, which was all I needed to persevere. After I told my father about my intention to study in Great Britain, I was glad to see he was supportive. My mother, too, even though she couldn't support me as much as she wanted to, due to her citizenship dispute.

— ∞ —

I needed to conduct some research on university applications, and I required a spot with reliable internet access. I turned to my stepdad and asked if he could take me to his office whenever he had a relaxed day at work. He worked tirelessly throughout the week, and even on weekends, as the editor-in-chief of a prominent newspaper. I recall feeling thrilled and curious as my stepfather escorted me, along with my younger siblings, to his workplace on a Saturday. Despite our having visited the office numerous times before, he decided to give us a tour of the building for the very first time, eager to show off the inner workings of his beloved establishment.

We made our way past the reception area and into the press division, where massive printing presses thundered as they churned out the next morning's paper. I could feel the floor vibrating beneath my feet and the heat of the machinery on my face. My stepfather explained the process of how the paper was printed, from the layout design to the final product.

Next, we walked through the circulation department, where stacks of papers were loaded onto delivery trucks and sent out to newsstands and subscribers. I could see the intricate system of sorting and packing, while my stepfather described the challenges of ensuring timely delivery, rain or shine.

We headed to the digital media department and there I was introduced to a team of tech-savvy individuals who oversaw the website and online content, which met the hi-tech standards of the early twenty-first century. The room was filled with screens and devices, and I could feel the energy and excitement of the team as they worked to keep up with the constantly evolving world of digital journalism.

Finally, we arrived at the heart of the newspaper office: the editorial department. Rows of desks were filled with writers, editors, and photographers, all working tirelessly to produce the best possible news stories for the paper. I could see the stacks of papers and files piled high on each desk, and the walls were adorned with framed photographs of past news events.

As my stepfather showed me around, I could sense the pride he felt in his team and in the work they produced. The newspaper office was a world unto itself, a place where news was gathered, stories were told, and history was made. For a moment, it seemed like I was part of something truly special.

Once the impromptu tour concluded, I knew that I couldn't waste any time browsing the internet for meaningless content. With the limited time I had, I had to submit several personal statements to a range of universities, in addition to filling out my applications. My brothers also found ways to occupy themselves – Ẹnítàn settled in front of the office television, while Wálé, like me, had access to his own computer.

After I had submitted my fifth application, I decided to approach my stepfather and inquire about what he was working on. He enthusiastically delved into the intricacies of journalism, and I found myself captivated by his words. I continued to ask him more questions, and he answered them all with great patience and insight.

Throughout the day, I was inspired by my stepfather's unwavering dedication to his work. He even took the time to assist me in correcting some of the grammar in my personal statements, which motivated me to research even more universities and submit additional applications. I was filled with gratitude for his support and guidance, knowing that he would always be there for me, offering advice and encouragement when I needed it the most. And then he said something that stuck with me.

"Remember, life isn't always about where you come from, it's about where you're going. But still... never forget who you are and where you come from."

Those words echoed in my mind as I filled out the rest of my applications. I was inspired and knew I could go anywhere in life I wanted to go. I sent off my eleventh application of the day, I checked on my brothers, and as the day was coming to an end, I realised how blessed I was to have yet another supportive father figure, as he smiled at us all and said, "It's time to go home."

— ∞ —

Applying for a UK student visa was not necessary for me, as my intended stay in the country was not solely based on obtaining a place at a university. I had long-term plans, and with my father's assistance, I was fortunate enough to obtain a right-of-abode permit. This permit, which granted me unencumbered residency in the UK, was tied to the validity of my Nigerian passport. Once my passport expired, I would need to renew both my passport and the right-of-abode permit.

With all the necessary documents in order, I methodically planned my trip to the UK. I got positive feedback and provisional admissions from about half of the universities I applied to, but of course they would ask for a deposit of the tuition fees, which cost more for international students. I would need to get to the UK and work hard to pay those fees. So, with all the necessary documents in order and a solid plan for financing my studies in the UK, my attention turned to finding accommodation with family once I arrived.

Even though my birth father and stepfather were the significant paternal figures in my life, and my grandfather who

I had lived with for most of my childhood was now gone, there were other uncles, older brothers, family friends, pastors, teachers, mentors, and so on that played a part in shaping my ideals of what it meant to be a father. Some of them even lived in the United Kingdom. One of those people, I had only known from a safe distance. He was carefree and reeked of alcohol and cigarettes most of the time. He had a way with words and a certain charm about him, but I never bought into his gimmicks like others did. I did observe him to be resourceful, and he detested the idea of working for the institutionalised establishments and hierarchies, always speaking about taking ownership, no matter the cost.

That person was Aunty Mimi's partner, Uncle Taj.

Uncle Taj had entered our lives as a suitor for my aunt but disappeared once she became pregnant, and fled to the UK. Aunty Mimi eventually gave birth to their daughter, Dámi. Rumours circulated that he had an estranged wife and other children and, in fact, had even fathered two more children in the same year Dámi was born. Long before any speculation or rumours surfaced, I'd always had an inkling as to something being off about him. Some kids just have those instincts about people, and I definitely did for him. With a nine-year age gap between us, Dámi became more like a little sister to me than a cousin. I was, in a way, very protective of her, and she was the first beneficiary of all I had learned from the male father figures in my life.

In the depths of my memory, I can still recall the day Aunty Mimi packed her bags and headed to the UK to confront Uncle Taj. She and Dámi had been living with my mother up until that point, and the rumours of Uncle Taj's multiple relationships, along with talk of his questionable actions, had spread like wildfire. But despite it all, Aunty Mimi couldn't stay away from him. She entrusted a three-year-old Dámi into my mother's care and promised to return soon. Days turned into weeks. Weeks turned into months. Yet, Aunty Mimi remained overseas for no justifiable reason.

It wasn't until much later that we learned the unsurprising truth: Aunty Mimi was back in a relationship with Uncle Taj, entangled once again in his web of deceit. Her originally planned stay of one month extended much past that time, soon resulting in her being pregnant with his child once again. As a toddler, Dámi was understandably distraught and felt abandoned by her parents. Even with my mother's loving care, it was difficult for her to comprehend why she wasn't with her parents. I felt a kindred spirit with Dámi, not just because our mothers were sisters, but most especially because we were connected by similar circumstances, such as being born out of wedlock and, at similar stages of our lives, longing for the presence of our fathers.

Uncle Taj promised my mother financial support for the upkeep of Dámi, to help with her costly private school education, but those were just empty promises from him. Instead, he attempted to smuggle Dámi into the UK illegally with a fake passport, a plan that ultimately failed and left a blemish on Dámi's future visa applications.

Despite all the drama, Uncle Taj and Aunty Mimi welcomed a new daughter, Jọlá, and continued to live together. Knowing all of this, I considered staying with them upon my arrival in London. It wasn't a perfect choice, but it was the best option I could think of at the time.

Chapter 6

As I sat in my little brothers' bedroom, the familiar sights and smells of my mother's home transported me back in time – back to the days of my childhood, when I was just getting used to the idea of having a stepfather and younger siblings. But in the moment, I was surrounded by half-packed suitcases and travel essentials scattered across the bed. My mother and stepfather had offered to take me to the airport, so I was at their home for the night. I glanced over at the scale on the floor and was reminded to make sure I weighed my bags, so they didn't exceed the weight limit for my flight.

Upon completing the task at hand, a sudden rush of memories flooded my thoughts, and I found myself overcome with nostalgia. With years gone by, I had finished secondary school, completed all the necessary university-entry-level exams, sometimes even doing them multiple times just to get better grades. I was ready.

As my stepfather came into the room to check on me, memories cascaded through my mind, almost overwhelming me with their force. "Do you remember teaching me how to tie my shoes?" I asked, a wide grin spreading across my face.

He chuckled in response. "Oh, I certainly do. You tripped over those laces so many times, but you never stopped asking for me to help you over and over again. I must have tied, untied, and retied your shoes countless times that day."

I laughed heartily, the memory as vivid as if it had occurred only moments ago. "Yes, and you taught me that even the smallest things can be overcome with perseverance and practice."

My stepfather's eyes crinkled in amusement. "I'm proud of the young man you've become. You've grown up to be ambitious, respectful, and honest. As I've always said, life isn't just about where you come from, it's also about where you're going. But never forget—"

I anticipated his next words and decided to interrupt him mid-sentence, mimicking his voice perfectly. "Never forget who you are and where you come from." I grinned, knowing full well how he loved to impart this wisdom to me.

He beamed at me, his pride in my achievements evident in his gaze. "You owe it to yourself to have strong role models in your life—"

"And I hope you know, evidently, you are one of them?" I rhetorically interjected, and he smiled.

My stepfather had taught me that it was okay to be vulnerable, even in a society that often discourages it, especially in men. I was entirely at ease opening up to him. But my train of thought was derailed when suddenly, he asked, "So, are you planning to stay in the UK long term, or are you coming back as soon as you are done with your education?" I paused for a moment, my mind racing to gather a response. The truth was, I didn't have a meticulously mapped-out plan for my future. I was still exploring, still discovering the paths that lay before me.

"Well, as you know, I have a one-way ticket. If I do come back, it won't be anytime soon," I said, with a lump in my throat. It had only just occurred to me how much I would miss him.

"You remember that famous John F. Kennedy quote? 'Ask not what your country can do for you – ask what you can do for your country.' Remember you can do a lot here too," my stepdad said. If I didn't know better, I'd say he was trying to convince me not to go. I mustered a chuckle.

"JFK was not thinking of the current state of Nigeria when he said those historic words," I said, restraining myself from wanting to go into political matters.

"Touché… Touché," he conceded, his voice carrying a mix of understanding and acceptance.

There was a light tap on the door. My mother poked her head in and smiled at us.

"Akándé mí, can you do me a favour?"

"Sure, Mum."

I raised an eyebrow at her, wondering what she wanted. As she entered the room, there was a large bag in her hand. "I need you to take a few things with you to London," she said, placing the bag on the floor. "Your aunty has been asking for some of our homegrown goodness."

I peeked inside the bag and saw a collection of goodies: blended melon seeds, yam flour, dried hibiscus flowers, and several packets of spicy beef jerky known as kilishi. "Mum, are you trying to make me exceed the baggage limit?" I protested, my eyes widening.

My stepfather chuckled. "Don't worry, Akándé. We'll make it fit somehow."

As we worked together to cram the items into my suitcase, my stepfather jokingly held up a tub of yam flour, pretending to weigh it in his hand. "I think we can only take half of this. It's heavy enough to bring a whole plane down!"

I gasped a little. My mother playfully swatted him on the arm. "Abeg don't tease him. He's already stressed as it is."

In the end, we managed to fit everything in without going over the weight limit. As we stepped back to admire our handiwork, my stepfather grinned. "Who said packing couldn't be fun?"

Ready to embark on my journey, I knew that the lessons my stepfather and other father figures had taught me would remain with me always. Their guidance and mentorship had played an integral role in shaping me into the man I had become, and I was deeply grateful for their influence.

On the day of my departure, as I said my final goodbyes to my stepfather and mother, a confluence of excitement and apprehension swirled within me. The journey ahead of me was long, and I wasn't sure what to expect. As we approached Murtala Muhammad International Airport in Lagos, the noise and chaos of the city gave way to an ambience of order and control. I could see soldiers and police officers in uniform standing guard, their weapons at the ready, providing reassurance of security amidst the flurry of activity.

I made my way to the baggage check-in counter, dragging my bags behind me. The crowds were overwhelming, and I felt like a small fish in a large pond. I became aware of the opportunists lurking about, trying to extort money from unsuspecting travellers – not uncommon to a Lagosian like myself, yet jarring to behold in an airport. I was relieved when I finally got through security and had my passport stamped, knowing that I was one step closer to my destination.

Boarding the plane, I was struck by the elegance and sophistication of the aircraft. Sitting in coach, a twitch of jealousy crept in towards the first-class and business-class passengers, who seemed to be enjoying a world of luxury and privilege. Nevertheless, I tried to make the most of my journey, watching movies, reading books, adjusting to high-altitude ear popping, and catching up on some much-needed sleep.

When the plane finally landed at Heathrow Airport, I was greeted by the biting cold of a November morning. As I made my way through baggage claim and immigration, the question of where I would be staying long term still lingered on my mind. Before my departure, I had informed my siblings of my flight itinerary, but they'd all seemed too busy to pick me up, so I then told Aunty Mimi, who was excited at the chance to collect me once I arrived. It had been years since I'd seen any of my older siblings, and the prospect of reconnecting with them felt both exciting and daunting. My father insisted that I spoke to all my siblings, broaching the idea that I lived with them temporarily until I could get on my own two feet. Those were the instructions I reluctantly agreed to because I didn't want to be a burden to anyone. But I was more excited to see Aunty Mimi.

Dragging my bags along with me, It felt like I was in a completely different world. The people, the levels of organisation – everything was so different from what I was used to in Lagos. As I walked out of the arrivals gate, I saw a little girl with a curly Afro, dressed in a bright yellow winter jacket, holding a sign with my name on it. *That must be Jọlá.* Right next to her were Uncle Taj and Aunty Mimi. As I approached her, she looked up at me with big, bright eyes and a shy smile, then quickly hid behind her mother's leg. But before I knew it, she was peeking back out, with a twinkle in her eye and a giggle that sounded just like her mother's.

On the way to the carpark, Jọlá chattered away about her favourite TV shows, her best friend at school, and the toys she couldn't wait to show me at home. She was talkative, but also a little hesitant, as if she wasn't quite sure if she could trust me yet. I could tell that she was a sensitive child, attuned to the emotions of those around her, but also curious and eager to make new connections.

When we arrived at her family's home. Jọlá took me by the hand and gave me a tour of the small, one-bedroom, government-subsidised East London council flat, while pointing to the sofa bed as where I would sleep. Aunty Mimi had helped tidy the corner of the living room as "my space", though I began to worry about the lack of privacy I would probably get in this small accommodation. Jọlá showed off her stuffed animals and her artwork proudly. She was still a little shy, but her eyes lit up with excitement as she told me all about her school life and favourite foods, which I wasn't surprised to find included some Nigerian delicacies such as pounded yam and ẹgusi soup – a soup made from ground melon seeds and often cooked with vegetables and/or meat, that has a rich and nutty flavour.

Jọlá struggled to pronounce my name; she had tried a few times since the airport, and I could see the discomfort and embarrassment on her face each time her parents would laugh at her attempts. I decided to make things easier for her.

"Akándé is pronounced ah-KAHN-day, with emphasis on the second syllable, 'kahn', but you can call me AK," I suggested with a smile.

Jọlá's eyes lit up. "I love it! And can I be Jewels? My friends in school call me Jewels."

I smiled. "Jewels it is. I think it suits you."

It was a small gesture, but our little nickname exchange made us forget we had just met each other that day. It made me feel even more at home in her flat. Despite her young age, I could sense that Jọlá was a thoughtful, introspective child, with a wide-eyed look of wonder. I was looking forward to getting to know her better and seeing how she would mature in the years to come. The confined space, however, had me a little hesitant, so I told my aunt and uncle that I would be going to stay at my siblings' homes over the next few weeks, promising to be back. I just wanted to get a feel for how my older siblings lived.

— ∞ —

A few days went by, and I was back at the front door of my aunt's council flat as I breathed a sigh of relief. The familiar scent of fried plantain filled the air, and the braggadocious hums of Fẹla Aníkúlápọ̀ Kútì's music played in the background. Aunty Mimi greeted me with a warm hug, offering a haven of comfort that I hadn't felt in days.

"You're back! So soon?" Aunty Mimi exclaimed as she pulled me into a tight hug. "How was your visit with your siblings?"

I sighed and took a seat on the worn-out sofa bed. "It was… overwhelming. Their homes are so different from what I'm used to. Both of my sisters' houses were like something out of a magazine, and my oldest brother's place… a very sophisticated mansion, where I half expected a butler would collect my coat at the door. But it's not just the material things, Aunty. Their lifestyles are so different from ours. They're all so focused on success, on making money, on fitting in with the English culture. I just don't know if I can keep up with that."

Aunty Mimi placed a hand on my shoulder. "Ah ah, they have gone the 'oyinbo' route, haven't they?" She let out a bit of a chuckle and went on. "I see you're going through a bit of a culture shock… Pèlè. You don't have to keep up with them, my dear. You're your own person, and your own journey is just as valid as theirs. Do you feel like you don't belong with them?"

I nodded. "Probably... Maybe all except for Kùnlé, who is the youngest of my four older siblings and lives a very modest lifestyle. But as for the rest, it's like we're from two different worlds. Plus, their kids – my nephews and nieces... there are so many of them, and they all have the latest gadgets and designer clothes. I can't keep up with that, Aunty, not to mention how hard it would be to keep up with all their birthdays, Christmases, and milestone events. I just feel so overwhelmed."

"That's understandable, naw. But remember, family is family, and we love them no matter what. You don't have to change who you are or be like them to love them. And you know you always have a place with us. You can stay here for as long as you need to, and we'll support you in whatever way we can."

I smiled at Aunty Mimi's words. "Thank you, Aunty. I think I've made my decision. I want to live with you and Uncle Taj and Jọlá. I just feel more comfortable and at home here."

Aunty Mimi's face lit up. "Of course, we'd love to have you, naw. And don't worry about the gifts and birthdays. We'll help you keep track of everything, won't we, Taj?"

Uncle Taj nodded from the kitchen, where he was nibbling on some plantain. "Of course, my boy. You're family, and the ties that bind us are unbreakable."

Relief flooded through me. It wasn't an easy decision, but I knew deep down it was the right one. I was ready to start my own journey, at my own pace, surrounded by the love and support of my aunt, uncle, and cousin. And who knew? Maybe someday I'd be able to bridge the gap with my siblings and their families. But for now, I was content to be where I was, surrounded by the warmth and familiarity of home.

Act III: Adulthood

"Lagos to London,
Culture shock shapes his young heart,
Manhood's path unfurls."
- Tòbí

Chapter 7

The cool London air hit me as I stepped outside my aunt's house, igniting profound excitement for the new school year as an undergraduate. On my way to my morning shift at the clothing store, I took in the different smells that filled the air: freshly brewed coffee, the scent of just-out-of-the-oven bread, and faint exhaust fumes from passing cars. It was all so different from the hustle and bustle of Lagos, but I was ready to embrace the change.

After work, I returned to my aunt's house to find Uncle Taj waiting for me. He challenged me about why I never bought groceries for the house. His question seemed unfair since I was saving up for university tuition fees, but I started restocking the fridge and kitchen cupboards whenever I got the chance after that confrontation.

Even though I had known him for years, there was always something unsettling about my Uncle Taj that I couldn't quite put my finger on. He didn't have a job, but he was studying political science at a nearby university to fulfil his political aspirations. Meanwhile, my aunt held the title of the breadwinner in the family, working as a carer for the elderly at a retirement home two hours away by train.

It was Jọlá's eighth birthday, and the little flat was filled with guests to celebrate the occasion. The tempting aroma of delicacies filled the air, and the birthday cake was already candlelit. As I opened the door to let more guests in, I was hit with a cacophony of noise – children's laughter, chatter, and movement all around me.

It took me a moment to register what I was seeing – a group of five children and teenagers, different ages and sizes, all introducing themselves to me. Three of them were Uncle Taj's children by his ex-wife, and two were from another woman. Their resemblances gave them away, and their faces were filled with joy and excitement as they made their way into the small living room which usually served as my bedroom in the night-time.

I couldn't believe it – these were Uncle Taj's children, the ones that were rumoured to have existed from his previous relationships. I stood there, trying to take it all in, but I couldn't shake the feeling that something was off. *How could no one have mentioned they were coming?* Aunty Mimi didn't seem surprised, or she probably had a good way of masking her true emotions. Either way, I didn't give the situation too much thought, and welcomed our new guests.

As the night wore on, I felt on edge. Uncle Taj seemed too pleased with himself, as if he had pulled off the ultimate deception, again something probably only I took notice of. The children were nice enough, but their presence was a reminder of the secrets and lies that seemed to be lurking beneath the surface of this family, secrets and lies that Aunty Mimi had tolerated and acclimatised herself to. I wondered what other secrets they were keeping from me.

Days passed, and my unease grew. One evening, Uncle Taj had some of his drinking buddies over and was particularly chatty, telling stories about his university days and his political aspirations. But as the night went on, the conversation took a dark turn. He started talking about his ex-wife, the mother of three of his children, how he had conned her into marrying him, just so he could get his papers and legal right to remain in the UK. The way he spoke about her was cold and calculating, as if she was nothing more than a means to an end. It was as if he had no remorse for what he had done to her, or to the children he had brought into the world.

I couldn't take it anymore. "How could you do that to her?" I blurted out. "How could you be so cruel?"

Uncle Taj's eyes turned red, and his gaze narrowed. "Ah ah, Kí l'odè? What's it to you? What's your concern?" he sneered.

"You are my concern," I said, my voice shaking with anger. "You hurt that poor woman, and you hurt those children. And I won't stand by and let you do it again to my aunty."

There was a moment of silence as Uncle Taj glared at me. I knew I had crossed a line, but I couldn't bring myself to apologise. His drinking buddies also fell silent and stared, not at me, but past me. I turned around to see Aunty Mimi standing in the doorway to the living room; evidently, she had overheard the conversation. The damage was done. From that moment on, the awkwardness and tension between me and Uncle Taj began to build with palpable intensity, and our relationship was never the same.

My undergraduate years went by very swiftly, and I had now paid off three years' worth of tuition fees – thanks to savings from my part-time job at the clothing store. I was on track for a second-class upper degree with a good grade-point-average, and my graduation day was on the horizon. I was already applying for ten jobs a day while attending at least two interviews a week, until I received an entry-level graduate job offer in user interface/user experience design – often referred to as UI/UX design – at a company located in central London. My very first tech job, months ahead of my graduation, in a profession that was highly sought after in the early 2010s. As soon as I got the start date for the job, I began making plans to get a place of my own, somewhere close to my aunt's home. The tension between me and Uncle Taj was still uncomfortable, and it was unsustainable for me to keep living there. Obviously, sleeping on a couch was never the long-term goal, but after over three years on that same sofa bed, I had kind of grown attached to it.

Embracing liberation and newfound independence, I bid farewell to my aunt's home of free food, free toiletries, and no bills, eagerly venturing out into the world of adulthood. I found myself a humble abode, a comfortable one-bedroom studio apartment, tucked away in a quiet corner of East London just two miles away from my aunt's home. The place wasn't the most luxurious or spacious, but it had everything I needed – a washing machine, a refrigerator, an oven, and even a communal garden where I could soak up the sun and tend to the greenery. But as I settled into my new home, the reality of adulting soon set in. With a graduate's salary on the horizon, I had to scrape by and make do with what I had. Furnishing my new space became a daunting task, one that required creativity and resourcefulness. Every purchase had to be carefully considered, every penny accounted for. And as the monthly bills piled up – electricity, water, and internet – I learned the hard way that financial responsibility was not to be taken lightly.

Despite the many challenges, I found solace in revisiting my former home from time to time, reminiscing about the memories I had made there. With every visit, I experienced a bit of pride in the journey I had embarked on, and how far I had come.

Aunty Mimi was acutely aware that her two daughters, despite their frequent video calls, still felt like strangers towards each other. After overstaying her visa for several years, Aunty Mimi finally resolved her immigration issues and announced her plans to journey to Lagos with Jọlá; my mother and Dámi were overjoyed at the news. The trip was a week-long, yet to Jọlá and Dámi, it seemed a fleeting moment compared to their lifetime of being apart.

Chapter 8

I stood in front of the full-length mirror in my flat, taking one last look at myself in my graduation gown. The black robe felt heavy on my shoulders, but I knew it was a symbol of all the hard work and sacrifices that had brought me to this day. I adjusted my mortarboard cap, making sure the tassel was on the correct side. I had been looking forward to this moment for months, excited to walk across the stage and receive my degree in front of my family and friends. Uncle Taj wasn't in the country, and neither were my parents, so I was only expecting Aunty Mimi and Jọlá there.

Just as I was about to leave my room, my phone rang. I picked it up to see a familiar number: Aunty Mimi possibly about to tell me they were on the way. But as soon as I heard the voice on the other end, my interest was piqued. It was Jọlá, using her mother's phone.

"Hello?" I said, trying to hide the concern in my voice.

"AK. Something's wrong with Mummy," she said, her words coming out in a rush. "She collapsed and she's not moving."

A knot formed in my stomach as I listened to her panicked voice. Of course, Jọlá thought to call me first because her dad wasn't around. I tried to remain composed, so as to help her stay calm. "Jewels, dial 999 to call an ambulance right now, and tell them what you just told me," I said firmly, trying to keep my voice steady. "I'm coming over."

I hung up the phone and rushed out of my apartment, not even bothering to take off my graduation gown. I ran down the street, feeling the wind whip through my hair and the gown flap behind me. I didn't even notice the strange looks from passers-by as I dashed past them. I hadn't passed my driving tests yet, so I had no car, but a bus ride would get me there in ten minutes.

I got closer to the block of flats, and as I got off at the bus stop, my heart raced. *What if something really serious happens to my aunt? What if there's nothing I can do to help?*

When I finally arrived, I saw an ambulance parked outside their house, with two medical examiners attending to Aunty Mimi. My cousin was standing on the pavement, looking lost and scared. I rushed over to her, dropping down to her level and putting a hand on her shoulder.

"Is Mummy okay?" she asked, her eyes brimming with tears.

"She's going to be fine," I said, trying to reassure her. "The ambulance is here to take her to the hospital for further observation."

I scooped her up in my arms and held her tight, feeling the weight of her small body against my chest. In that moment, my graduation ceremony felt like a distant memory. All that mattered was being there for Jọlá and Aunty Mimi.

As we watched the ambulance pull away, an aura of calm settled upon me. My aunt was in good hands, and my cousin was safe with me. We would get through this together, one step at a time. I had informed Uncle Taj and my mother of the incident as well through separate phone calls. As soon as we got all the details from the hospital, Jọlá and I went to visit. It seemed Aunty Mimi had been coughing incessantly just before her collapse. But what we thought was just a cold turned out to be more severe. And then came the diagnosis – she had a lung disease. She would soon be discharged, but over time, she would be forced to quit her job due to the demands on her health. The once-vibrant woman who had taken care of us all was mostly confined to her bed, struggling to breathe, and only able to walk very short distances.

$$- \infty -$$

Regrettably, there was more peril on the horizon. The council flat that had once been our home was now under threat. Uncle Taj had not been paying the rent for over six months and had intentionally been ignoring bailiff letters and warnings. It was puzzling because this council flat's rent was subsidised by the government, and Uncle Taj only needed to pay fifteen percent of the market rate. Aunty Mimi had been oblivious to the warnings until one day, while she alone was at home, a bailiff came in person, banging on the front door to hand-deliver the eviction notice to her. It was a waking nightmare.

And then came the final blow. Uncle Taj, in his desperation to save their home, had attacked and hurt my aunt because she wouldn't lend her signature to a fraudulent claim to retain the flat. She had called me on the day of the incident, while I was at work, and I made my way to their flat as soon as I could. I could still see the bruises on her arm and the fear in her eyes. It was like all the trust that we had in him had been shattered. The once-reliable man had become a monster in the eyes of his family. The house that was once filled with laughter and joy was now silent and tense. When I confronted Uncle Taj about the incident, he made light of the issue, and I told him we would have to report the case to the police, to which he responded with nonchalance.

We went to the nearby police station, and Aunty Mimi issued her written statement. Soon enough my aunt's breathing problems began to escalate again; she struggled and made very strained efforts to move around. Aunty Mimi, irrespective of her pain, remained determined in her resolve to not get knocked down in these dire circumstances, and kept a brave face on for Jọlá. On our return from the police station, Uncle Taj was still there in the flat, sitting on the sofa, watching TV. He showed neither acknowledgement nor remorse as I guided my aunt and Jọlá, with all their packed-up suitcases and boxes, out of the flat they had lived in for years. They were never going to return. It was the day before the bailiffs would come to kick everyone out of the house, so I asked Aunty Mimi and Jọlá to stay at my place indefinitely, while I moved most of their things into paid storage. That night, I volunteered my bedroom to my aunty and cousin, who reluctantly accepted my offer. I could see in my aunt's sickly eyes that she felt both shame and gratefulness, but I paid no mind to her feelings of embarrassment and made her feel more than welcome. As I lay on my leather sofa bed, I closed my eyes and took a deep breath, wishing I could pray away the events of the day.

The next morning, we sat around the table, eating the breakfast that Jọlá had helped me make, while awkwardly trying to avoid conversations about the previous day's events. I could feel the burden of concerns and uncertainties weighing Aunty Mimi down. The smell of my aunt's medicine filled the air, and seeing her barely eat her food made her frailty more apparent than ever before. She clung to her little girl's hand, her eyes filled with a mix of fear and exhaustion. Jọlá looked up at me with big brown eyes that sparkled with careless wonder. The excitement of sleeping over in her big cousin's flat was a good enough distraction for her. *It must've been like a mini-vacation for her,* I thought. I could only imagine how her little mind would process surviving the physical and emotional abuse she had witnessed between her parents.

Despite my aunt's ill health preventing her from working, Jọlá was still able to attend school, and thankfully her school was a few minutes' walk from my flat, so she was able to make her way back and forth on weekdays. For the next six weeks, my aunt and Jọlá lived with me. My mother, who was in Lagos, called every day to check on them. Jọlá was full of energy and always optimistic. My aunt, on the other hand, due to the springtime cold, spent most of her time resting under blankets, unless she absolutely had to go out. When she did go out, it was with Jọlá, to the London council housing agencies to seek support with shelter, and soon enough, they were eventually offered a place in Luton, just outside London. I packed their things and helped them settle into their government-funded accommodation. Jọlá made friends with the other children in the area, while my aunt relied on government benefits. I made sure I checked in frequently, as Luton was just under forty-five minutes' drive for me at regular driving speed. My aunt also made friends in the area, and they were supportive of her condition and circumstances. One such friend I did get to meet. Her name was Lárà, she had two daughters of her own and just happened to be a nurse. Lárà being a nurse came in handy, as she provided Aunty Mimi with a lot of health-related assistance and advice, seeing as she worked at the local hospital Aunty Mimi was registered at. She also helped babysit Jọlá, along with her own kids, when my aunt had to make short trips to the hospital. Jọlá started fresh at a new school, which coincidentally was the same school as Lárà's daughters'. It's a miracle Jǫlá was still able to maintain good school grades at the time, whilst going through so much.

— ∞ —

Time flew by in a blur, and they grew accustomed to life in Luton. Aunty Mimi depended on government aid to keep her head above water, paying her bills and putting food on the table. Unfortunately, her health gradually deteriorated, and she became a frequent visitor to hospitals. To ease the burden, Lárà would collect Jǫlá from school alongside her own children, take her in to sleep over, then get her ready for school again in the morning, for the next few days. When Aunty Mimi's hospital stays stretched out longer than anticipated, she was deeply grateful for the assistance. Every weekend, I visited her in the hospital, bringing Jǫlá with me after fetching her from Lárà's place. Seeing my aunt tethered to a drip was gut-wrenching. It was heartbreaking to witness her suffer so much, but Jǫlá was always on hand to lift her spirits and put a smile on her face. The hospital staff were well acquainted with Aunty Mimi, as she was a frequent patient under their care. It was no secret that Lárà was close to Aunty Mimi and often looked after Jǫlá. As a result, Lárà was listed as the primary next of kin, with my name as the secondary contact.

"Akándé, jǫ́. Promise me something." Aunty Mimi's feeble voice cut through the jovial atmosphere of one evening at the hospital, her request laced with an urgency that accentuated her sickly demeanour. She implored, her serious tone underscoring the gravity of her words.

I paused, unsure of what she was about to ask, but I chose to assume it was nothing existential. "What's that, Aunty?" I asked.

She leaned in, her words meant only for my ears. "Promise me, no matter what happens to me, you won't let Tajúdẹ́ẹn take Jọlá," she said, her words barely above a whisper. "I don't think I have much time left. Everything hurts."

I tried to interrupt, offering words of affirmation and prayer quotes, but she cut me off. "You're not listening," she said. "I'm literally dying. You, more than anyone else, know how many times I go in and out of hospitals. I'm asking you to be prepared, in case Tajúdẹ́ẹn wants to take Jọlá away. Aside from you, your mother, and Lárà, there is no one else I trust with taking care of her. And your mum lives in Lagos, and Lárà, bless her heart, has done more for me than I could ever request. So, promise me. Promise me you will protect Jọlá from him."

I swallowed hard, the weight of her request heavy on my shoulders. "I promise, Aunty," I said, hesitantly. It wasn't that I was unwilling to protect Jọlá – far from it – but I was hesitant to accept that Aunty Mimi had given up on her life. I knew she was in pain, but the thought of losing her was unbearable.

As the evening wore on, the laughter and chatter faded away, replaced by a sombre mood. I couldn't shake the feeling that Aunty Mimi's time with us was running out. The enormity of the request weighed heavily on me. I found myself wondering how anyone else would fare in dealing with such a daunting task. But for the moment, I tried to push those thoughts aside and cherish the time we had left together. Though thankfully, a few weeks after our dialogue, she was feeling better and was discharged.

On Christmas Eve, having made plans with Jọlá and Aunty Mimi to spend Christmas Day together, I went to bed with the same frenzied excitement I'd always had every Christmas Eve before that day. My aunt, who was back in the hospital again, had originally been scheduled for discharge earlier that week but encountered a few complications from an endoscopy procedure, leaving her with scarring that meant she had to stay longer. That did not deter me from my plans. The next day, I was scheduled to make my way to Luton, pick Jọlá up from Lárà's house, and spend the day with them in the hospital, bringing along some food and snacks. But at 12:15 am, in the middle of the night, I received a frantic call from Lárà.

"Akándé! Akándé!" Lárà screamed over the phone.

"Hello, Lárà, Merry Chris—" I was interrupted by her panic.

"I just got a call from Luton and Dunstable Hospital. They say Mimi is gone. I can't leave the kids at home, are you able to go to the hospital?" she said with a shaky voice.

"What do you mean she's gone?" I sought to clarify.

"I don't know the details, Akándé, but they said she choked and…" Lárà paused for a second. "She choked and died. I can't go, please can you come?"

"Okay, I'll be on my way. What about Jọlá?" I asked curiously, wondering if she knew as well.

"She's still asleep. And I really don't think I have the courage to be the bearer of bad news either. This is too much," she lamented, her voice breaking, and it sounded like she was about to tear up.

"It's okay, I'll tell her," I muttered, attempting to be reassuring. "I'll be at your place as soon as I'm done at the hospital. See you soon."

I drove as fast as I could to Luton, tears streamed down my face, whilst a tremor of dread crept up my spine. Christmas already felt ruined forever. So many thoughts were racing through my mind, and I probably committed many speed limit violations on my way. I quickly arrived at the hospital, and I was told it was a sudden set of repeated coughs that left her gasping for air that had led to her death, in spite of how hard the nurses and doctors tried to revive her. I saw her warm body lying there. I hovered, not knowing what to do. I could see the familiar tip of her scar peeking just above the neckline of her shirt as I held her hand one last time, while the thought of breaking the news to everyone else crossed my mind. Experiencing another death in the family was overwhelming, and I wasn't sure how anyone would bear the pain or react to it. But in that moment, I was numb.

Leaving the hospital, I made my way to Lárà's house, where I found Jọlá sitting under a towering and twinkling Christmas tree with the other kids. I summoned her to step outside with me, informing her that I had something important to share. She followed me into my Honda Civic, and I drove her to her mother's flat in silence, dodging all her inquiries about her mother's health. We parked the car in front of the house, and I broke the news to her gently, though the words weighed heavily on her tiny frame.

"I'm really sorry, Jewels."

I held her close, feeling her struggle and cry, knowing I had to be her anchor through the turbulence of grief. Irrespective of the fact that I couldn't save my aunt, I had to be there for Jọlá, to remind her of the love that still existed in her world.

"Promise me!" Aunty Mimi's words echoed in my head.

The sudden heaviness of the responsibility of being her father figure and potential legal guardian weighed on me, even though I knew that I could never replace her real father. The thought of a custody battle made me queasy, but I knew I had to do everything in my power to keep her safe and sound. As I stared out of the car window, I struggled to come to terms with the depth of my loss, and the sudden weight of my newfound responsibility.

Chapter 9

On Christmas morning, I reached for the phone with a heavy heart to break the tragic news to my mother. But as I began to dial her number, a sudden realisation hit me like a bolt of lightning. Her twin, her parents, Aunty Ìyábò, and now her dear little sister had all passed away, leaving her as the lone survivor of that once thriving nuclear family.

Summoning all my strength, I took a deep breath and recounted the events of the past twelve hours to my mother. As soon as I told her, she let out a deafening scream that echoed through the phone, revealing her unpreparedness for such a tragedy on Christmas Day.

Her pain reverberated in a quiet static on the call. Unable to speak, my mum handed her phone to my stepfather, who pressed for more details.

"What did the doctors say?" he asked stoically.

I replied, "They said it may have been due to the lingering effects of an endoscopy procedure. She coughed repeatedly and then choked until she passed out." I had become numb to the effect of recounting the gory details.

"Your mother will be flying over to the UK as soon as possible to help you out." Hearing that from him was a bit of a relief, because I was starting to think this was going to be too much to handle alone.

Soon enough, I had to speak with Dámi. But as soon as I heard her voice, I realised how similar it was to her mother's, and I started to miss Aunty Mimi all over again. Dámi's voice trembled with emotion. She was bargaining with the universe, desperate to find a way to come to the UK as soon as possible. But her previous attempts at obtaining a visa had been met with one obstacle after another, each one sending her further into despair. And then anger took hold of her, a fiery emotion that burned as she lashed out at the thought of her father, blaming him for ruining her chances of being closer to her mother. It was as if the anger gave her some raging control in a world that had suddenly become so uncertain. But just as quickly as the anger had come, denial crept in, a cold and cruel intruder that refused to let her accept the reality of her mother's passing. Dámi clung to the hope that maybe, just maybe, her mother was still out there somewhere. Yet despite the tumultuous emotions that raged within her, there were moments of acceptance in her voice. She knew that she had a duty to her little sister, Jọlá, and she embraced that responsibility, even as the physical and emotional distance between them seemed insurmountable. But as the call drew to a close, she began to sound cold and distant, wanting just to be alone. I did worry and hoped that she wouldn't become reclusive or depressed. I was left reeling, stunned by the intensity of Dámi's grief.

Everyone expressed their condolences. My father and older siblings empathised with me through phone calls and text messages, compassionate about the unbearable pain that I was experiencing. Additionally, even strangers from Luton whom I had never met before shared kind words about Aunty Mimi. The one person I wasn't ready to talk to was Uncle Taj. He had been calling my phone, but I chose to ignore him. I already knew how that conversation would go. I knew that Uncle Taj wouldn't take this with ease and grace. He had a reputation for being manipulative and controlling, and I was sure he would try to use Jọlá as a pawn, even in this heightened state of grieving. But I was prepared to fight him, no matter what it took. Even if it meant going to court, I was determined to protect Jọlá from his toxic influence.

While sorting through Aunt Mimi's belongings at her Luton flat, I prepared for Jọlá to move in with me – the weight of the responsibility rested heavily on my shoulders. Uncle Taj had tried to get in touch with me through other mutual contacts as well, but I still chose to ignore him. I knew that he would try to intimidate me, but I remained resolute. I wouldn't let him bully me into giving up Jọlá.

I had heard rumours that Uncle Taj didn't even have a home, and that he was planning to use Jọlá to leverage government funding for housing. It sickened me to think that he would stoop so low, but I was determined to do everything in my power to protect my little cousin.

It wasn't going to be easy, and I knew that the road ahead would be full of obstacles and challenges. But I was ready to face them head-on, for Aunt Mimi's sake, for Jọlá's sake, and for my own. I owed it to them to be strong and steadfast, no matter what.

Just a few days before New Year's Day, my mother arrived in London, and Jọlá and I went to pick her up from the airport. We could see the redness in her eyes behind her glasses, evidence of her grieving state. She played an essential role in reaching out to our extended family members, who provided much-needed financial support for the funeral. With that taken care of, Jọlá, my mother, and I settled into my studio flat.

About a week after my mother's arrival, rain had been lashing down all day long, but that did not stop my mother,

Jọlá, and I from heading to the local store to buy a few things. Once done, we carried our bags of groceries, holding up our umbrellas while we made our way back home, when we noticed a police car parked on the kerb very close to my flat. There were two policemen in the car, watching us intently. My heart began to race as we hastened our steps into our home.

Just as we walked in and locked the door behind us, I started to count from ten to one in my head, trying to calm my nerves. *Ten, nine, eight, seven, six, five...* But before the countdown ended, there was a knock on the door. No surprise, it was the police.

They showed me a court order as they stood at the entrance, and I started reading through the document. My mood plummeted as I read that Jọlá had been declared "missing" and that we were considered a flight risk, and that her passport needed to be seized. The document also made outrageous false claims about my mother performing female genital mutilations on little girls in Nigeria and that Jọlá would be her next victim. I could feel the anger boiling inside me as I continued reading.

I protested, telling the police that they needed an actual search warrant to come into my home. But they forced their way in, flinging the front door wide open. Before I could react, they handcuffed me against the wall. I could hear my mother and Jọlá screaming, but it was like I was in a daze as my face was actively pressed and bruised against the wall. The incident attracted the attention of the neighbours, who gathered outside, recording the whole thing on their phones. It felt humiliating and degrading to be treated like a criminal in my own home.

My mother quickly showed the police the documents from social workers, which stated that I'd been granted temporary parental responsibility for Jọlá. Only then did they de-escalate and uncuff me.

86

This was clearly Uncle Taj's despicable attempt to take his daughter away from me, and he had gone as far as declaring her missing to the authorities. I knew it was all a ploy, a vindictive scheme to get back at me for standing up to him. *How on earth does he know my mother is in the country? Why would he call her a genital mutilator?*

In a fit of suppressed rage, still feeling the strain of my cheekbone from being pushed against the wall, I blurted out, "You do realise a child needs to be in the care of a parent before they can declare that child missing, right? This girl has not seen this man in person for almost two years."

One of the police officers retorted, "We are just doing our jobs and following the court order's mandate." Then he continued, "Also, if his name is on the child's birth certificate, then he has parental right to ask for his child."

I didn't completely agree with the police, but I chose not to argue. Luckily, because the social services documentation specifically stated that Jọlá was not in any danger staying with me and my mother, the police became more lenient, but they still demanded Jọlá's passport, which I gave to them reluctantly. The police placed us under semi-house arrest until the court date, which meant we could go out, but none of us, especially Jọlá, could spend the night anywhere else. We would be under some sort of surveillance. The police attempted to confiscate my Nigerian passport as well, but fortunately I had already sent it off as part of my British passport application, and I presented the application details to prove this to them. The police, incorrectly sensing desperation on us, issued a stern warning against renewing Jọlá's passport as a means of escape from the country. The thought hadn't even crossed my mind. Their presumptions made my skin crawl with unease, and their instructions of confinement felt suffocating, as if the walls of my flat were closing in around us. The neighbours breathed a sigh of relief on our behalf. We were left with nothing but our thoughts, our fears, and the ever-present weight of problems stacking on top of each other. As the police left, I could see the smug looks on their faces, like they had gotten the better of us. But I knew better. This fight wasn't over yet. This was the worst kind of tug of war yet – one with Jọlá caught in the middle.

As I recovered from the encounter, my mind slowly became consumed with thoughts of potential medical malpractice that may have led to my aunt's untimely demise, and how the system just wasn't working in our favour. I knew I needed to tackle this issue head-on. I knew I had to seek professional legal advice regarding both medical investigations and child custody laws.

During my time at the hospital, I was asked to fill out bereavement documents, coupled with signing forms granting permission for medical examiners to take my aunt's body to the morgue in preparation for an autopsy. Despite feeling uneasy about the situation, I'd completed the necessary paperwork.

I couldn't shake the feeling that something was not right. A few weeks before her passing, my aunt had expressed her concerns about the doctors scarring her throat during intubation, despite her not fully consenting to the procedure that led to the scarring. In spite of being hesitant, she'd still gone through with it, only to lose her voice and experience the repeated coughing fits that eventually led to her death.

— ∞ —

After a few days, the autopsy was finally completed, and a death certificate was issued. I was shocked and outraged to say the least. It was clear that there was a discrepancy, and I knew that I had to take action to ensure that justice was served. The section on her death certificate with the cause of death details stood out to me, and went as follows:

Cause of Death for Abídèmí Adébáyọ̀
Categorisation of Death: Natural causes

The precise cause of death was as follows:

1a Aspiration of blood
1b Iatrogenic hypopharyngeal tear
2 Ventricular septal defect (previously operated on)

I had to conduct some research of my own, seeing as how the medical examiner might have been trying to throw off suspicions of any foul play. A simple internet search of these technical words would reveal a lot more detail.

Blood aspiration occurs when blood is breathed into the lungs (going down the wrong tube). It might happen during choking, but aspiration can also be silent, meaning that there is no outward sign.

Iatrogenic means a complication that happens to a person after getting medical treatment. Iatrogenesis is the causation of a disease, a harmful complication, or other ill effect by any medical activity, including diagnosis, intervention, error, or negligence.

Hypopharyngeal tear/perforation is a rare complication of endotracheal intubation. It most commonly occurs at the hands of a less experienced physician in emergency situations. The site most commonly perforated is the pharynx, posterior to the cricopharyngeal muscle; the second most common site is the piriform sinus.

Ventricular septal defect (VSD) is a birth defect of the heart in which there is a hole in the wall (septum) that separates the two lower chambers (ventricles) of the heart. This wall also is called the ventricular septum.

As I read through the coroner's statement and death certificate report for Aunty Mimi, frustration rattled me. We had already known that the birth defect mentioned had been treated when she was a baby – it was clearly documented in her medical records. So why was the medical examiner acting as if they had uncovered some shocking revelation?

Despite my annoyance, I couldn't dwell on it for long. The aspiration of blood and iatrogenic hypopharyngeal tear only added to my suspicions that something wasn't right. I knew I had to take action.

I filed a plea with the hospital's bereavement centre, determined to initiate a coroner's inquest. This was the first step towards getting the answers we needed and uncovering the truth about what really happened to my aunt. I knew that it would likely lead to a court hearing, but I was willing to take that risk.

On the other hand, the cost of hiring a lawyer to represent me was astronomical. Between the expenses of the funeral arrangements and potential legal fees for a custody battle, my finances were already stretched thin. It seemed like everything was working against me.

But I refused to give up. This wasn't just about money or personal gain – it was about seeking justice for a loved one and ensuring that no one else would suffer from such negligence. I was determined to do whatever it took to bring closure to this situation, even if it meant sacrificing my own financial stability.

Moving my aunt's belongings out of her old flat and preparing for Jọlá to come live with me only added to the mounting pressure. And the constant worry of an attack from

Uncle Taj made things even worse. Despite everything, I knew I had to stay strong for Jọlá and honour my aunt's dying request. No matter what, I had to be there for her.

The funeral was a solemn affair, with only a handful of well-wishers present. The sound of the wind rustling the leaves of the trees that lined the graveyard was the only audible noise. Aunty Mimi had always said she wanted a low-key send-off, and we respected her wishes. Standing next to my mother and Jọlá, I watched as the casket descended into the freshly dug earth. My eyes followed it down, and a lump formed in my throat, threatening to choke me to tears. It was difficult to accept that my beloved aunty was gone forever. The weight of my grief was suffocating, like a leaden blanket draped over my entire body.

Jọlá stood beside me, her face a mask of inexpressive stoicism. I wondered if she fully grasped the enormity of the situation. She was so young, and this ordeal might leave a lasting impact on her psyche. My mother, on the other hand, was inconsolable. She wailed uncontrollably, unable to hold back her tears.

The funeral director's advice to have a closed-casket service was difficult to accept, but we understood the reasons. The corpse was not in the best condition for a public display, and we couldn't bear to see her in a state that wasn't dignified. My mother was especially unhappy that she couldn't see her sister one last time. Dámi couldn't make it due to visa issues, and I sent her pictures throughout the service. Jọlá's father was not invited for obvious reasons. We didn't need any extra drama on this sombre day.

As the coffin disappeared into the ground, my mother's crying became louder, and it started to feel like I was losing her too. With Aunty Mimi's passing, my mother's guttural wails must've been triggered by a sudden realisation – that she now was the only one left alive of all her original set of siblings and parents. The cumulative weight of those losses seemed to be crushing her soul. I knew she would have to leave for Lagos soon, leaving me alone to take care of Jọlá. The magnitude of responsibility felt overwhelming, but as I took Jọlá's hand, I knew I had to be strong for her. I had to be the father she needed. It was my promise to Aunty Mimi, and I intended to keep it.

Act IV: Fatherhood

"Unplanned fatherhood,
A promise to keep with love,
Guided by grief's light."
- Tòbí

Chapter 10

My aunt had always been there for me, even when nobody else was. I remember when I was nine years old and I fell from a tree in my grandparents' garden, breaking my left arm in two places. Aunty Mimi had left her one-month-old daughter, Dámi, in the care of my grandmother and driven me around Lagos in search of a hospital that would take me in. It was Easter Monday, and most of the hospitals had a shortage of medical personnel. So rather than wait for an ambulance that didn't exist in 1990s Lagos, she drove me around until we found a suitable hospital to admit me to. I remember the excruciating pain, but I also recall the comfort in her arms.

As I tried to navigate the legal complications of my aunt's passing, I was compelled to think back to that day. The fear and uncertainty of not knowing if I would receive proper medical care, and the comfort of having my aunt by my side. Now, I was faced with a different kind of uncertainty. The legal battle over the potential medical malpractice that had led to her demise, and a child custody battle over Jọlá. There was a third legal conundrum too, one to do with my application for British citizenship. Though the one that seemed the most personal would have to take a back seat to the other matters at hand. In need of guidance, I consulted my father, a barrister-at-law himself, about how to navigate my complex situation. Our conversation was fruitful, and I made sure to act upon many of the points he had given me. At the time, one of my older brothers, Kùnlé, had plans to get married in London in a few weeks. He had asked me to be one of his groomsmen, to which I'd excitedly agreed. My father was in the UK, staying at Kùnlé's home for a time. I went to visit them to get details of the wedding outfits from Kùnlé, in addition to getting some much-needed legal advice from my father.

"Make sure you collate as many relevant documents as you can. Every single one of your aunt's old documents that you acquired from her home could be useful in your case. Supportive witness statements could also go a long way," my father advised.

"Thank you, Dad. I will. However, I'm worried that one of the court dates might clash with Kùnlé's wedding. I already told him, but he thinks it'll all work out in the end." I expressed my unease.

"Hopefully, it does work out. You should be focusing on getting married like your brother. Do you even have a girlfriend?" my dad inquired.

"No, I don't."

"You know what, I think I may have the perfect person for you. Do you remember my friend, Dr Coker? Well... he has a daughter I think would be perfect—" Dad said, as I began to interrupt his insistent verbal momentum.

"Gosh, Dad, no. Not one of your matchmaking recommendations again. Remember when you tried to set me up with a relative?"

"You were not related," he interjected.

"Well, not by blood, but if it's my stepmother's niece you were peddling my way, then think of how awkward it would be for my siblings to have me, their brother, in a relationship with

96

their cousin. I think that's a little incest-adjacent, don't you think?" I argued.

"Fair point," for a man who argued for a living, he conceded a little too quickly.

"Plus, right now, my priority is getting custody and taking care of Jọlá. It's what her mum would have wanted," I went on. My father rolled his eyes at me, as though I were making petty excuses.

"Well, if things don't work out, you can always send her to an orphanage, a foster home or something. You should focus on yourself," he remarked offhandedly.

"Dad, that's not a nice thing to say," I retorted, disappointed.

"I was just kidding," my father said, trying to backtrack and regain my favour. "Where's your sense of humour?" But it was too late. He had already worded his thoughts, and those words made me feel a mix of distaste, disbelief, and disappointment.

My aunt's passing had added to the already considerable burden of caring for my mother and Jọlá in my London flat. The expenses of arranging her funeral and providing for my loved ones had drained my finances to the point where affording legal representation seemed impossible. My father's guidance was all I had, but the stakes were high, and I knew it wouldn't be enough. The complexity of the legal system demanded the expertise of a law firm to help me collate the evidence that came from myself, witness statements, and social services.

Dipping into my meagre savings was my only option to secure justice for Jọlá, and it would only cover a mere three hours of a lawyer's time. Those precious hours would be essential in the initial court hearing, where I would need the expert guidance of a legal representative by my side.

I could feel the weariness of all my worries bearing down on my shoulders as I clutched my nearly empty wallet. The future was uncertain, but I knew I had to keep fighting, keep pushing, keep advocating for Jọlá's right to a stable and loving home.

The day of the pretrial came upon us quickly. My mother, Jọlá, and I made our way to the courthouse. Irrespective of the effect on her school attendance, Jọlá's presence was mandatory, and she was summoned particularly to be assessed by two middle-aged women – one a child psychologist and the other a social care worker. They took her away into a playroom right opposite the courtroom, so she would feel comfortable, distracted by the toys, while they got the truth out of her. I was quite certain they asked her questions like:

Do you miss your mother?

Do you want to go live with your father?

Is your cousin safe to be around?

Do you have a room all to yourself?

What does he feed you?

Have you been attending school since your move back to London?

My mother and I sat next to the doorway of the kids' playroom where Jọlá answered questions. Then, all of a sudden, he appeared, gallantly waltzing in even though he was late. It was the first time I had seen Jọlá's dad in a while. He looked well. But even though I had tried to acknowledge him in the moment, as he sat down five metres away, adjacent to us, he completely ignored me and my mum. My mother and I shared a quick knowing glance. Trying to say hello felt awkward. Soon enough, Jọlá came out of the room with both ladies. She immediately saw her dad, glanced at my mum and me, as if seeking approval. I nodded, and Jọlá ran to hug her dad. She had clearly missed him. This was the first time she had seen him since the eviction. That was almost two years prior. The child psychologist took some notes, in response to what she was observing between daughter and father. I felt a bit like a villain. To a third party who had no context or background to the situation, I was the relative keeping a daughter away from her father. But such was the quandary I found myself in. Either I kept the promise to my aunt, or I washed my hands of the matter and left Jọlá to fend for herself with a conniving father. He wasn't a perfect man, but he was her father all the same. After their long embrace, and him asking after her wellbeing, she left him and came to my mother and me.

The pretrial hearing was about to begin, and because Jọlá was too young to be in the courtroom, she would have to wait with the social care worker and the psychologist. The law firm I was working with had sent over a lawyer, just for the initial proceedings. Unfortunately, my initial payment to them would not cover the cost of a lawyer for subsequent hearings, just the pretrial. My mother shared a few reassuring words with Jọlá as we left her with the social worker and walked into the courtroom. Our lawyer introduced himself to us at the door and motioned for us to sit towards the left side of the room. Jọlá's dad headed towards the right side of the room.

As I stepped into the courtroom, a tingling sensation of anxiety came over me. My heart was pounding in my chest, and my palms were sweaty. I took one last look over at Jọlá, who wasn't allowed in the courtroom. I heard the social worker say, "She'll be fine with us, not to worry, sir."

I nodded towards the lady and gave Jọlá a reassuring smile. In between our shutting the courtroom doors and walking over to our seats, my lawyer gave me some last-minute courtroom etiquette.

"You shall refer to the judge as Sir or Your Honour. You shall only address the judge if he addresses you directly. You shall under no circumstances be interruptive – let me do the talking on your behalf for the most part," the lawyer warned.

"I 'shall' comply," I responded sarcastically. He responded with a wry smile; he wasn't amused at my attempt at humour. I had only met this lawyer for the first time that day, so in an attempt to cut the tension in the room, I thought I'd poke some fun at him.

"Mr Jímọ̀h, can you please tell me what you do for a living?" The judge's voice interrupted my thoughts.

"I am a UI/UX designer, sir... I mean, Your Honour," I replied as I stood up to address the judge, trying to keep my voice steady.

"And do you earn enough to take care of a prepubescent child?"

"Yes, Your Honour. I do."

The judge nodded. "And do you live alone?"

"I usually do, Your Honour. But currently, in addition to Jọlá, my mother, who is visiting for my aunt's funeral, is staying with us."

The judge raised an eyebrow. "What are your long-term plans for Jọládé Dàdá?"

"To protect and care for her, Your Honour. To ensure she gets an education. To move into a bigger home, where she has a room to herself."

The judge called my lawyer towards the bench to ask him a few questions. After a brief exchange, the lawyer presented a document to the judge and returned to his seat. The judge turned to me.

"And how do you intend to accommodate Jǫládé's father into her life?"

My lawyer chose to respond on my behalf. "Your Honour, visitations can be arranged. Even so, my client would very much like to keep his promise to the child's mother, to protect Jǫlá from her abusive father."

"Thank you, counsel, but I would like to hear from the defendant," the judge interjected. "Do you, Mr Jímǫh, have written proof of this so called 'promise'?"

"No, Your Honour, this was conveyed verbally to me by my aunt," I responded with a bit of concern, fearful things weren't going my way.

"So, why would the mother see you as a better guardian than the child's father?" the judge asked, seeking clarity. I turned to where Uncle Taj sat alone, without a lawyer of his own, and turned back to the judge.

"Your Honour, for almost two years, Jǫlá's father did not go to visit this child. I visited Jǫlá and my aunt every two weeks after they got evicted. I used to live in that same house too. He hurt my aunt, and she was a victim of domestic violence." My lawyer flips through his folder of documents, pulls out a sheet of paper, and takes it to the judge. I take a deep breath and continue.

"Your Honour, my aunt became terrified for her life, and of the negative influence he could exert on Jǫlá. That is why the housing association recommended my aunt move far away from him. She trusted me because, like my mother, she had known me all my life and could vouch for my character as a good influence for Jǫlá." I was out of breath. My voice was beginning to shake. The judge gestured for me to take a seat, while he continued to take down some notes.

The judge then turned to Uncle Taj. "As claimant, you have petitioned the court, requesting to have your daughter live with you – is that correct, Mr Dàdá?"

"Yes, Your Honour," he replied.

The judge continued. "Where do you currently live, Mr Tajúdẹ́ẹn Dàdá?"

"I live at 8 Mill Road, CB11 3LB."

"And who do you live with?"

"I currently live with my partner and our two sons."

The judge looked at his records. "Do you have any other children?"

"I have other children, Your Honour, including Jọlá."

The judge asked, "When was the last time you spoke to or saw either Jọládé or Jọládé's mother?"

"About a year ago. I called frequently, but she wouldn't let me see my daughter. So, I sort of lost contact after some time."

The judge frowned. "You don't sound very persistent, Mr Dàdá. Are the allegations about domestic violence against you true?"

"Your Honour, it is my humble opinion that those allegations are grossly exaggerated," Uncle Taj replied.

"There is a detailed police statement here, written by the deceased, stating, and I quote, 'he squeezed my neck' and 'he pushed me' and a number of other allegations. Are these false, Mr Dàdá?"

"Again, Your Honour, grossly exaggerated." Uncle Taj remained adamant in his response.

"The home you currently reside at, under whose name is this property registered?" the judge inquired.

"It is registered in my partner's name," Uncle Taj responded in a nonchalant manner. A court official cautioned him to address the judge as "Your Honour".

"It has been documented, as well, that you have another daughter with the deceased. Is that correct?" the judge queried.

"That is correct, Your Honour," Uncle Taj answered without hesitation.

"She is named Oh-lah-dah-mee...? Oh-luh-dah-mee-lair...? Oh-loo-dah-mee...?"

The judge adjusted his glasses as he struggled to read Dámi's full name off the piece of paper in front of him. In a rare moment of shared amusement, light reproach, and solidarity, Uncle Taj, my mother, and I all said in unison, "Olúwádámilárè!"

"But you can refer to her as Dámi, Your Honour," Uncle Taj said.

"Thank you, Mr Dàdá." The judge moved on swiftly. "And am I correct in saying that it's the defendant's mother who has cared for your other daughter, Dámi Dàdá, in Nigeria for more than a decade?" the judge asked, sounding like he had a few more questions in the chamber.

"Yes, Your Honour. Dámi has lived in Nigeria all her life. We've been trying to get her over here, but we have faced several roadblocks to this endeavour."

My mother let out a huge sigh in the court, signalling her disagreement with Uncle Taj's statement.

"So is Dámi a victim of female genital mutilation?" the judge quizzed Uncle Taj.

"Not to my knowledge... I don't believe so," Uncle Taj waffled in response.

"Then why did you say the defendant's mother was an active female genital mutilator, if she already takes care of one of your daughters?" The judge cornered him with his words.

"I think my statement was taken out of context. I said, 'She was taking Jọlá to a country with a high likelihood of female genital mutilation', not that Akándé's mother conducts them," Uncle Taj unconvincingly attempted to clarify.

"I have a written statement here. This one is from you. In your writing, and it says 'I believe my daughter is unsafe and in danger with her maternal family. They are known for their involvement in female genital mutilations,'" the judge pressed. "Strong allegations here. Care to clarify?"

Uncle Taj said nothing.

The judge continued to take down some notes.

The judge then revealed that he would allow for optional visitations at a neutral location once every two weeks. Uncle Taj was visibly disappointed; he protested but maintained his composure. Knowing him, he would be too proud to initiate fortnightly meet-ups with Jọlá and me, unless Jọlá decided she wanted to see him.

The judge declared that before the next hearing, I would need to arrange an inspection of my home with the designated social worker to ensure it provided suitable living conditions for Jọlá. I would also need to make sure she attended school, agree in writing to visitation rights for Uncle Taj, then formally apply for both special guardianship and parental responsibility for Jọlá. I agreed to all the court's demands. The court pretrial session came to an end, and the trial was scheduled for a later date, in about a month. My mother departed for Lagos the weekend after the pretrial. So, it became just me and Jọlá again.

— ∞ —

The next week, however, was the court case to challenge the suspected medical malpractice. I had no funds for a lawyer, so I had to face the judge myself.

As I stepped into the courtroom, I was struck by its appearance. It looked more like a conference hall than a traditional courtroom. The walls were adorned with sleek wooden panels, and the large windows at the back allowed the natural light to flood in. The high ceiling with ornate chandeliers added to the grandeur of the room. I had expected the courtroom to be a place of solemnity and gravitas, but instead, it felt cold and impersonal. The benches for the audience were made of polished wood, with the upholstered seats looking more comfortable than the stiff wooden chairs I had seen in movies. The judge's bench was a large, imposing structure at the front, and the witness stand was to its right.

Looking around the courtroom, a twinge of anxiety crept up my spine. The thought of standing in front of the judge, without a lawyer to represent me, made me feel vulnerable. I took a deep breath and walked towards the witness stand, where I was supposed to make my case. As the judge entered the room, a sudden strain of concern washed over me. I knew that I had a strong case, however the thought of the medical professionals who had caused my aunt's death walking away unpunished made my blood boil. But as the proceedings began, my frustration gave way to disappointment. The defence was quick to belittle my aunt's death as inevitable, and I began to feel a cloud of despair hovering over me.

"She had a complicated medical history, and the professionals tried their best to restore her to optimal health," the one lawyer stated; a dismissive tone laced his words. "It seems to me that had they done nothing up until the point of intubation, her situation would possibly have worsened. Also, the non-resuscitation at her collapse was strategic so as not to cause any accidental damage to her already precariously compromised lungs."

The judge tried to reassure me that I had the option of appealing the decision, but I knew that I was too defeated and exhausted to take that route. The courtroom with all its grandeur felt like a mockery of justice. A deep chasm of disillusionment with the legal system engulfed me, and I knew that seeking clinical negligence compensation from the National Health Service would not bring my aunt back from the dead. All I wanted was accountability from those who had overseen her life. I couldn't stand hearing random strangers referring to my aunt as a mere cadaver. I hadn't even grown accustomed to referring to her in the past tense, yet these court individuals had no qualms talking about her like a distant memory. She deserved better... As I left the courtroom, I questioned if justice had truly been served.

— ∞ —

Time had flown by since the custody battle pretrial, and the day for the main trial was here. As I walked into the family court, my hands were shaking with anticipation. Jọlá's presence wasn't required on the day, so she was at school, safe and sound. I was ready to face Uncle Taj once again. But to my surprise, he was a no-show, and a wave of elation swept over me.

As the court granted me full custody of Jọlá, a mix of emotions gushed through me. On the one hand, I was thrilled at the prospect of being able to provide a stable home for my adoptive daughter, but on the other hand, I couldn't shake the nagging feeling of guilt. Would keeping Jọlá away from her father harm her in the long run?

Despite my doubts, I was officially granted special guardianship and parental responsibility, and a profound mix of wonder and disbelief struck me. *Me? A parent?* It was a daunting prospect, but I was determined to do whatever it took to give Jọlá the life she deserved. The life Aunty Mimi would've wanted for her.

Leaving the courtroom, I stepped out into the warm orange glow of the setting sun. My mind was still racing, but this time with relief and determination. I couldn't wait to see Jọlá and share the good news with her. Thankfully, I could still make it to my brother's wedding, which was happening later that evening, so I had to pick her up from school to get ready. *It will be nice to catch up with the rest of my siblings at the ceremony as well,* I thought. As I walked towards Jọlá's school, my heart swelled with love and gratitude. It was the start of a new chapter for us. The smells of freshly cut grass and blooming flowers tickled my nose as I walked past the sound of children laughing and playing football in the school field. I made my way to the front of Jọlá's classroom, and as soon as she saw me on her way out, her eyes lit up with anticipation.

Without a word, I pulled out her passport from my pocket, a physical representation of the good news I had to share. Jọlá's eyes widened in amazement, and then a huge smile spread across her face. She ran towards me, arms outstretched, and I scooped her up in a hug.

We both laughed, caught up in the moment of joy. It was a small victory, but it meant the world to us. And in that moment, I revelled in the feeling of being able to provide Jọlá with a small glimpse of hope and freedom amidst the most tumultuous of times.

Chapter 11

My courtroom dramas seemed like they were over, but not all my legal battles were won yet. There was still the worrisome matter of my citizenship and domiciliary status. The right-of-abode I had entered the country with alongside my Nigerian passport was still not as powerful or as affirming as a British passport, especially if I saw myself staying in the UK long term. I needed a British passport.

A few years prior to Aunty Mimi's passing, I'd sent in an application for a British passport, with details stating that I was entitled to such a claim to British citizenship through my parents. My African parents, one of them born in the UK, albeit with a disputed identity, and the other a naturalised citizen. Soon enough, I was called into the passport office for an interview.

The interior was modern as expected, with sleek silver panels and bright lights that illuminated the otherwise sterile surroundings. I took a deep breath and walked towards the front desk, my heart pounding with nerves.

As an immigrant or expatriate, depending on how such statuses are categorised, I had been warned that obtaining a British passport was a notoriously difficult and lengthy process. It was common knowledge that my current Nigerian passport held a lesser and unfair reputation globally, particularly when it came to visa-free travel. For that reason, I longed to be a UK citizen, free from the travel, living, and working restrictions that came with the documentation I had in my possession.

I had done my research and prepared fastidiously for this interview. I had brought all the necessary documents, filled out the forms with care, and rehearsed my answers to the potential questions. But still, a haze of uncertainty and apprehension lingered in the back of my mind.

As I waited for my turn, I looked around at the other applicants. There were people of all ages, ethnicities, and backgrounds, all hoping for the same thing as me. Some looked confident and composed, while others appeared nervous and uneasy. I mulled over the chance that they might be feeling the same way as I was.

Finally, it was my turn. I approached the interview room with a mix of excitement and trepidation. I sat down and smiled at the interviewer, hoping to make a good first impression. My heart was racing, my palms were sweaty, and my mind was in a thousand different places. The session felt more like an interrogation than an interview. I was questioned, probed, and made to feel like a criminal because of my impression of entitlement. They also spoke about my mother.

"How do we know your mother isn't the identity thief in this disputed matter?"

I couldn't believe the insults I was getting, all for wanting to be recognised as a citizen of the country I had legally lived in for several years. Of course, I was aware you had to legally live in the UK for a minimum of five years to initiate the process of becoming a naturalised citizen, but I was hoping it would be easier to claim through my parents. Clearly, I was wrong.

As I took the train and walked the familiar streets leading home on that day, I thought about the journey that had brought me to that point. It had been a long and arduous one. But I had never given up. I had always believed that I was entitled to British citizenship by lineage, and I was determined to fight for it, despite the outcome of that first interview. My mother's identity theft had led to a major nitpick in an unblemished application process. My father had always taught me to stand up for my rights. He had instilled in me an understanding of justice and a desire to fight for what I believed in. Typical lawyer dad. His words always inspired me to take on the system. I had pleaded my case at the interview, trying to be eloquently convincing in my not-so-British accent. But, of course, I was denied. It was a much bigger fight than I had anticipated, and I was facing a monolithic system. What I didn't realise at the time was that, as a result of my initiating that first meeting, the Home Office would open a file on my behalf that would flag any future applications linked to my name, not in a very good way.

But I had a contingency plan. I followed the guidelines judiciously, even did a "Life in the UK" test to prove I had grown accustomed to the way of living in the UK, and sent off my application for naturalisation. Within weeks, I got my naturalisation certificate and a handshake from a government official. It felt like I was getting closer. Subsequently, I sent a second application for a British passport, with my newly collected naturalisation certificate and Nigerian passport. This second application for a passport was met with radio silence. A silence that cost me many months of not being able to travel due to not having a passport, or even being able to change jobs due to lack of identification. My father wrote to the passport office about the matter so many times on my behalf that he even threatened to take them to court.

— ∞ —

After six months, which was just a month before Aunty Mimi's passing, I received an official letter inviting me for yet another passport interview. This felt ominous, but I tried to stay optimistic. I prepared for the meeting and informed my family, who provided all the support they could. As I walked into the small room for my passport application interview, I saw two people seated on the other side of the plexiglass barrier. These individuals were different from the people I'd met at the first interview. At this interview, the older man had a harsh face and an imposing air about him, while the younger lady seemed more amenable, and she looked like she was only there to observe.

"Good morning," I greeted them, trying to sound as polite as possible. The older man just looked at me over his glasses, while the younger one gave a small nod. I could feel my nerves creeping up on me.

The interview started off with the usual questions, but soon enough, the older man brought up my mother's identity theft case. "We have reason to believe that your mother's identity was compromised," he said, staring at me intently. "What do you know about this?"

I explained to him that my mother had indeed been a victim of identity theft and that we had taken all the necessary steps to report it. Yet he continued to press me on the matter, insinuating that I was somehow involved.

Next, the validity of my naturalisation application was questioned. They wanted to know if I had ever been in trouble with the law and if I had any ties to extremist groups. I remained calm and collected, knowing that I had nothing to hide. The barrage of accusatory questions continued, but I never let my composure slip. Even though the older man's tone was biting and condescending, I answered every question truthfully and with confidence.

Finally, they told me that the documents I had brought with me were not enough to grant me a passport. I couldn't believe it. They had asked me similar questions as they had my mother when she went to the British consulate in Nigeria to challenge her identity theft. She had told me she had been fighting tooth and nail for years, but all for nought.

The whole experience left a bad taste in my mouth. As I was dismissed from the premises, they made copies of my documents. I knew that I had to formulate another contingency plan to get my passport.

A mix of frustration and anger coursed through me. I couldn't help but wonder if this was just another form of discrimination. But I refused to let it get me down. Something inside me refused to give up. I knew I had to fight for my rights, even if it meant going against a system that was bigger than me.

The seizure of my naturalisation certificate by the British passport office, along with my Nigerian passport and all other personal documents, left me stuck in a frustrating limbo. All I had was an outdated driver's licence, which didn't even show my current address, making my only form of identification questionable. I remained steadfast in my belief that I wouldn't be stuck in this limbo forever. I cultivated the habit of visualising manifestations, printing off copies of British passport covers available on the internet and believing they were a physical representation of what I desired.

One day, after Jọlá was settled and living with me at my place, I received a letter from the "Status Review Unit – Deprivation and Revocation Team", threatening me with deportation and deprivation of my entitled domiciliary rights. I was given a twenty-one-day ultimatum and an opportunity to give a convincing response as to why I deserved to maintain my naturalisation and be issued a British passport. The letter listed several demands, including providing evidence regarding my mother's confirmed identity. Explaining fully why her identity was disputed. Explaining in full why I applied for naturalisation as a British citizen if I already had a claim for British citizenship by descent by virtue of my mother's birth in the United Kingdom. And finally, explaining why I chose to follow my father's advice that "it was easier to obtain British citizenship through him."

I put my thinking cap on and went to work on doing some research. There is a disturbing fact about the legitimacy of citizenship by descent in the United Kingdom, which is colloquially referred to as the "children of unmarried fathers" rule. Or as I like to call it, the "bastard clause". Historically, a person did not become British if the parents were not married at the time of the child's birth. Legislation had now been passed to allow a route to nationality for those who were disadvantaged by the old version of that legislation, Section 50(9) of the British Nationality Act 1981, which had thankfully been recently revoked. The same twenty-one-day ultimatum letter tried to deny me my passport by enforcing a repealed law. *Ridiculous,* I thought.

I brought it up with my dad. He did some research as well, and referred me to a recent court case, which had to do with a man who was born in Jamaica, moved to the UK at the age of four with his Jamaican mum to live with his British dad, but remained legally Jamaican the whole time. His parents too were never married. He was then being considered for deportation as a result of him committing a knife crime when he was twenty-three years old. The judge ruled against his deportation, as his lawyers invoked this same legislation change that could now grant citizenship to descendants through their fathers. And my mother's case, legally, should not in any way have held me back. Based on this new information, I drafted my response letter, cited the case file, and rewrote it several times for my father to review until he felt I had covered every angle worth covering.

In addition to all of this, I quoted Articles 6, 7, and 8 of the Human Rights Act:

Article 6: Right to a fair trial. I mentioned this to prepare myself for the possibility of a hearing. Failure to present a compelling argument in my response letter could result in the denial of my opportunity to appeal against a potential deportation.

Article 7: No punishment without law. This was my rebuttal to the "bastard clause". They couldn't deny me what I was entitled to, based on a law that had since been reformed and revoked in my favour.

Article 8: Right to private and family life. I mentioned all my older siblings, nephews, and nieces who were British citizens, as well as Jọlá, Uncle Taj, and my cousins as the family ties I had in the UK. Granted, I had family in Nigeria too, but I was now the parent to my adoptive daughter, Jọlá.

I mailed my response. Four days later – add that to what felt like a lifetime – I received another letter in the post, asking me to make a third application and saying that this time, I would be granted the passport. The letter literally said:

Dear Mr Akándé Jímọ̀h

Having reviewed your petition, your citizenship via naturalisation will not be revoked and you will need to submit a new application for a British passport before it can be issued to you. Your other supporting documents will be returned to you separately.

Yours faithfully

UK Status Review Unit – Deprivation and Revocation Team

I filled out the paperwork and sent my application off. I eventually got my Nigerian and newly minted British passports within two days. It was a small piece of documentation, this passport, but it represented so much more. It was a recognition of my identity, my right to be here. I vowed to myself that I would do everything in my power to spare my future children from enduring the same ordeal. In retrospect, I'd remained resolute in my determination to see the process through to the end. I'd spent sleepless nights praying, meditating, and fasting, my anxiety visibly manifesting in my shaking hands and racing heart. But in the end, all my persistence and faith paid off.

Ironically, the same day I received my passport, I got back home, switched on the TV, and caught sight of a news clip featuring refugees struggling to cross borders on overcrowded dinghies, battling against the rough waves of the ocean to find safety. The poignant scene stirred up strong feelings of empathy within me as I imagined the harrowing journey and hardships they must have faced.

Their unwavering determination to seek a better life and secure their freedom despite the odds was both inspiring and heart-wrenching. As I watched the refugees bravely forge ahead, a stark reminder came over me. A reminder that we all share a common desire for a better life and deserve the autonomy to pursue it, no matter where we come from.

Chapter 12

I sat on the edge of my bed, staring out the window, lost in thought. I glanced over at my dream journal on my nightstand and realised that I had not logged any dreams in weeks; I was either not dreaming, forgetting to log them, or forgetting I had dreamed at all. The past few months had been rough. Playing daddy-dearest was no easy job, but I saw myself as up to the task. My mind felt like a battlefield, constantly at war with itself. I was still sitting at the edge of my bed, my mind racing with thoughts that refused to let me sleep. My cousin snored softly on the sofa bed in the living room, her breaths a reminder of my own precarious living situation. I looked around my one-bedroom flat, taking in the details that I had grown so accustomed to. The faded paint on the walls, the creaky floorboards, the small kitchenette in the corner. All of it seemed so suffocating.

I needed a bigger home. A place where my little cousin could have her own room, instead of sleeping on a sofa bed in the living room. I remembered staying at her parents' house not that long ago, even back then longing for space and freedom of my own. I wanted that for her, for both of us.

But my thoughts didn't stop there. I thought about my failed business that I had barely gotten off the ground, the African-textile-inspired wristwatch business that crashed and burned. I'd poured my heart and soul into it, but when my aunt passed away only a week after launching it, I couldn't give the business the attention it required. And now, I couldn't dissociate those watches from my grief, and I was left with nothing but debt and regret.

And then there was my job. A nine-to-five UI/UX designer job that served only to pay the bills. I spent my days crafting digital experiences that were intuitive and seamless. My fingers would dance over my keyboard as I painstakingly crafted mock-ups and prototypes. Sitting in a noisy office space, barely able to focus as I carefully selected fonts and colours that evoked the desired emotional response from users, continuously testing and tweaking the interface until every pixel was in its perfect place, creating a beautiful, functional design that delighted and satisfied both the user and the client. But all that monotony didn't fulfil me. I didn't want to spend my life working in a corporate setting, chasing someone else's dream. I'd much rather pursue my own passion projects, something that made me feel alive and content, than sacrifice my mental health and peace of mind.

I picked up my phone and dialled my mother's number, my fingers trembling slightly. I didn't know how to broach the topic directly, but I knew I needed to talk to someone. Most families never discussed or warned of the mental toll of life's trials and tribulations. Mental health was never addressed, not in my family, not in African families in general, and it left me feeling alone.

"Akándé mí, how are you?" My mother's voice interrupted my thoughts, as I hadn't heard the dial tone stop ringing. I nodded, as though she could see me, and then realised it was a phone call and I would need to speak up.

"Yes, Mum. I'm fine," I responded. "Just a little tired." We continued with pleasantries, catching up on family matters. She mentioned that there was some extended family staying over. Relatives I vaguely remembered. But there was one I did remember, the son of one Aunty Wùrà. The son was in his twenties now. We weren't close, but we were cordial. His mum, meanwhile, was out of the picture, and no one really spoke about her. It was like she dropped off the face of the earth. I hadn't seen her since I was a kid.

"Whatever happened to Aunty Wùrà, Mum? No one really talks about her. I do remember you were close."

"You know, you're right. Wùrà went through some really rough times," she said, dropping her voice down an octave. "She walked out of her house one day, leaving her young son alone, and never came back. No one has seen her since. It was a challenging time for our family, but we learned the importance of seeking help for mental health issues."

I listened to her story, feeling relief that I wasn't alone in my struggles. But at the same time, I was angry that these things were never discussed. *Why were we only ever told about the good things in life and never warned about the bad?* I wish someone had talked to me about stress, depression, and even suicide when I was younger, at least in a way proportional to my level of comprehension at that age.

"I know, Mum," I said, finally finding my voice. "It's just frustrating that these things are never talked about. I feel like I'm always walking on eggshells when I try to bring them up."

"I know it's not easy, but we have to do better," she replied. "Especially for those looking up to us."

Her words resonated with me, and I welcomed the responsibility of breaking the cycle. I knew I couldn't change the past, but I could make a difference in the present.

Just before that call ended, my mum didn't forget to tease me about not having a girlfriend, and I returned a jokey jab

119

right back at her, teasing her for her desperation for grandchildren.

"Don't be a womb-watching wedding-worrier mum! Haha! Love you... Bye!"

As I listened to her voice on the other end of the line, I found comfort in pouring out my heart and soul, telling her everything that'd been weighing heavy on my mind. And even though she didn't have all the answers, just having someone to listen helped ease the burden a little bit. That call was more helpful by the end than I'd realised it would be at the start. I took a deep breath and made a promise to myself. I would seek the help I needed, not keep things to myself, and without question, take better care of my mental health, even if it made me nervous and uncomfortable. I didn't want to end up like Aunty Wùrà, lost in the darkness with no one to turn to. I am all for breaking the silence and having uncomfortable conversations. I was a single father. I hated my job. My dating life was in shambles. I was twenty-five at the time, and had been unsuccessful in relationships throughout my early twenties. I couldn't seem to shake off my fear of commitment, a fear instilled in me by the men I grew up around. My introverted personality didn't help matters either, as I was often accused of being disinterested or aloof. But even though from a relationship standpoint, I was alone, the love of my own company ensured I never felt lonely.

As I sat in church one Sunday morning, I couldn't stop myself from noticing her. By her, I mean Shèwà. Shèwà was the complete opposite to me. I was an introverted person who found it such a chore to be social. But her energy, her extroverted personality, was magnetic. She belonged to the church's ushering department, and I would occasionally catch glimpses of her in action, handling tasks with ease and confidence.

It wasn't until a few months later, during a church Christmas party for young singles, that we finally spoke. As we played charades, Shẹ̀wà and I connected over our shared love of movies and music. Our conversation flowed effortlessly, and by the end of the night, we had exchanged contact details.

"I hope there's no one else named Shẹ̀wà on your contacts list," she said as she prepared to leave.

"Even if there is, I'll put the number one next to your name, because from today, you're my number-one Shẹ̀wà," I flirted. Or attempted to. She giggled. A win.

"Let's meet up again soon," she then said.

I smiled. "Definitely. Let's get together soon."

We quickly scheduled our next meet-up. I nervously adjusted my shirt as I waited for Shẹ̀wà outside the restaurant. It was our first date and I wanted everything to go perfectly. As she walked up, I became entranced in her beauty. Shẹ̀wà had glowing dark skin that seemed to reflect the evening sky, and her supple lips were just begging to be kissed. Her natural brown hair was intertwined into dreadlocks that flowed down her back, and her slightly awkward walk made her even more endearing.

As I approached her, she gave me a warm smile. "Hi!" she said, her voice filling me with zen. "You look great."

"Thanks. And you smell amazing, by the way," I uttered nervously as we shared lingering eye contact, just before I broke it by leaning in for a hug.

As we entered the restaurant, I observed Shẹ̀wà looking around, taking everything in. It was clear that she was a logical thinker and very pragmatic in her assessments. Despite being an extrovert, she was quiet around strangers and people she wasn't familiar with, but very outspoken with those she was comfortable with. I was grateful that I fell into the latter category.

As we sat down at our table, I could see that Shẹ̀wà was taking in every detail of the restaurant – the décor, the menu, even the cutlery. She was very observant, though a little impatient when it came to the waiter bringing her food. Her impatience was something she fully admitted to working on. It was one of the things I loved about her – her admission of her flaws and her commitment to work on herself.

Over dinner, we talked about our hobbies. Shẹ̀wà was a beautician on the side but worked full time in a bank as an investment banker. She loved gaming, movies, and travelling – all things that I was also passionate about. We laughed and shared stories, and before we knew it, the evening had flown by.

As we walked out of the restaurant, Shẹ̀wà turned to me with a smile.

"I had a great time," she said. "We should do this again sometime."

I couldn't agree more. It felt like I had found someone who understood me, someone who shared my interests and passions. As we said goodbye and went our separate ways, I knew that this was the beginning of something special.

As Shẹ̀wà and I got to know each other better, I realised that our compatibilities were undeniable. I told her very early on about Jọlá and how I became an "accidental" father. We had open and honest conversations about our goals, desires, and aspirations. She even got along well with Jọlá. We were becoming a team, supporting each other's dreams.

The "womb-watchers" and "wedding-worriers" were on my case, constantly asking me when I was going to settle down and start a family. And while I wasn't desperate to be with someone, I knew the value of having a partner in life. Shẹ̀wà and I had our fair share of obstacles and conflicts, but we always worked through them together. I've come to believe that compatibility is key, and that it takes all four elements – logical, emotional, spiritual, and sensual – to create a lasting bond.

Looking back, I realise that my journey with Shẹ̀wà wasn't always smooth sailing, but we persevered. Soon enough, she got to know Jọlá, and thankfully, they got along very well.

"Jewels is like the little sister I always wanted," she said about Jọlá once. Their rapport warmed my heart.

— ∞ —

Following the path of tradition, my family embarked on the Introduction Ceremony – a precursor to our much-awaited wedding day. At the bride's family home, to underscore our intentions as the groom's family, we arrived bearing gifts and a decorative "letter of proposal," revealing our aspirations for an enduring union. In kind, the bride's family bestowed upon us an ornately adorned "letter of acceptance," meticulously crafted with exquisite ornaments. Both gestures symbolising the profound extent of our families' commitment.

As the long-awaited day finally arrived, the air brimmed with excitement, infusing the vibrant Engagement Ceremony with energy. We donned colourful matching outfits crafted from the traditional handwoven fabric known as aṣọ oke, with separate designs for the guests and ourselves – the bride and groom – thereby adding an extra layer of glamour to the splendid occasion. The event was adeptly guided by two hosts – *Alága Ìjọkọ̀* and *Alága Ìdúrò* – who presided as the masters of ceremonies for the day. Within this celebratory ambiance, we exchanged symbolic treasures that resonated deeply: wedding rings, kolanuts, palm wine, and a cherished Bible. The tying of the knot ensued, binding our wrists with a cloth that echoed our unity. As we slipped on our rings and shared sips of palm wine, our unyielding devotion was sealed. With that, our families were united.

With humility and reverence, my friends joined me in a sincere prostration before the elders, while Shẹ̀wà and her friends would afterward kneel down in front of the same elders – a gesture seeking the blessings and prayers of those that came before us.

Gifts flowed, embodying the essence of kinship. *Eru Ìyàwó* – gifts from my side of the family – intermingled with treasures bestowed by the bride's family. Later, we would be seated regally on our throne-like perches, as guests approached us to offer blessings and seize the opportunity for photographs. Adorned in the splendour of Yoruba traditional attires, our families radiated the grace of age-old customs.

Naturally, a wedding is incomplete without a grand feast – an array of delectable party foods and drinks graced the scene. Guests indulged in a buffet of culinary delights, making their selections from the tempting offerings on display. Although I do admit to spotting a few naughty guests from a distance, stealthily whipping out takeaway bowls out of nowhere, all in the pursuit of securing that extra bit of food to take home. The air was filled with the rhythmic beat of talking drums, the harmonious melodies of praise songs, and the graceful movements of dancing, accompanied by the jubilant yet extravagant tradition of spraying money, until it covered the entire dancefloor.

As I reflect on my wedding day, I recall the significance of blending cultural traditions with Christian values. Being of

Yoruba heritage, it was important for Shẹ̀wà and I to honour certain cultural norms.

Though unconventional for "parents of the groom", especially for those with two parents, one of my top priorities was having all four of my parents – my mother, father, stepmother, and stepfather – present at the ceremony, taking centre-stage in matching outfits. Shẹ̀wà and I opted to write our vows and recite them to each other, a decision that I cherish to this day. I can still recite both her vows and mine word for word, and the memory of that moment remains etched in my mind. Mine went like this…

These are my vows to you.
I love and cherish you:
Your mind, body, and spirit.
You give me reason to be a better man every day.
My heart belongs to you.
Every one of your dreams, goals, and aspirations have now become my dreams, my goals, and my aspirations.
We will build an empire and conquer the world together.
You are my lover, my friend, and my confidant.
I promise to never keep anything from you, and I would fight endlessly to keep winning your trust and affection over and over again.
Our love will know no bounds; I will commit myself to you.
When there is darkness, I will be your light; when you need motivation, I will be your drive.
If we ever lose all our material possessions,
I know having you will be all the treasure I need.
You bring out the best version of me, and I promise to bring out the best in you.
You are so perfect to me.

You are perfect because your gorgeous eyes reassure me
not to worry, and that everything will be alright.
You are perfect because you give me a reason to be
happy every day.
You are perfect because I can love, trust, and rely on you
unconditionally, in good times and bad.
You are perfect because you are kind, patient, and you
accept me the way I am.
Just like a missing puzzle piece, you complete me.
I adore you, my wife, my love, my African queen.
I can't wait to make memories and spend the rest of my
life with you.
I am yours, and you are mine.
I promise to always love you,
From this day, until my last day.
These are my vows to you.

And hers went a little something like this:

It's crazy thinking how you came into my life
and fit in a way only God could have designed.
You are what I prayed for in my silent whispers to God.
I couldn't have put it into words even if I tried;
He knew the desires of my heart, even the ones I couldn't
put into words.
He knew just what I needed.
I promise to love you,
to be your biggest cheerleader,
a partner that will never stop challenging you as you
challenge me to be the best.
I offer myself to you as I am,
with all my flaws and all my strengths,
safe in the knowledge that you complement me perfectly.

I trust in you and in us completely,
physically, mentally, and spiritually,
in faith and in love.
I will listen, and when you're weak I'll pray for your
strength.
I will respect you, honour you and our marriage at all
times.
I will walk in love, patience, understanding, and grace.
I will hold your heart with integrity and love, and I will
stand with you.
Marriage isn't easy or perfect, but I know our union is
purposed – we are meant to be together.
I can't imagine anything I couldn't love you through.
I can't wait to spend the rest and best days of my life with
you.

My wife had never seen me cry, and I was not going to give the wedding guests the satisfaction of watching me turn into a sobbing mess. But if I'd heard her vows with no one else in a room, just us two, I probably would've found it hard to fight back those tears.

Soon enough, we planned on moving into our new home, and I was finally able to bid farewell to my cramped studio apartment. Jọlá, who had never had her own room since her mother passed away, would now have the luxury of a bedroom space all to herself.

On the day we successfully completed the purchase, we walked through the door of our new home, and I was immediately struck by the warm and inviting atmosphere. The sunlight filtered through the windows, casting a golden glow over the polished hardwood floors and pristine white walls.

Our new home was a four-bedroom semi-detached house on the outskirts of London, and we were all eager to explore every nook and cranny. As we walked through the airy hallway, I could hear the sound of birds chirping outside and the rustle of leaves in the gentle breeze.

Jọlá was jumping up and down with excitement as we showed her to her bedroom. She was overjoyed to have her own space, having spent almost two years sleeping on a cramped sofa bed. I could see the delight on her face as she explored every inch of her new room, from the vibrant turquoise walls to the soft, plush carpet underfoot.

As we continued the tour, Shẹ̀wà and I admired the spacious living room, complete with a cosy fireplace and a comfy sofa. The kitchen was a chef's dream, with gleaming stainless-steel appliances and an enormous granite countertop. I could already imagine the delicious Nigerian delicacies we would cook together in this welcoming space.

The bedrooms were equally impressive, each with its own unique charm and character. The primary bedroom had a luxurious en-suite bathroom with a deep soaking tub and a glass-enclosed shower. I pictured the long relaxing soaks Shẹ̀wà and I would enjoy after a long day at work.

Outside, the garden was a verdant paradise, with lush green grass and vibrant springtime flowers blooming everywhere. I envisioned our summer barbecues and lazy afternoons spent lounging in the sun.

As we finished moving all of our boxes, bags, and furniture in, a flicker of joy glowed within me. Our new home was the perfect place to start our new life together, especially with good train lines, shops, schools, and parks just a stone's throw away. The cherry on top for me was seeing the happiness on Jọlá's face; it made our move feel all the more special.

Around the time of our move, Jọlá began going through a growth spurt and becoming a hormonal fifteen-year-old girl, while developing some bad habits along the way. She was quickly growing into a pretty young lady; despite this, she still had some self-image insecurities, like being dissatisfied with her appearance. Insecurities that came with the standards of beauty set by peer pressure. Jọlá also took a turn as she started telling bold-faced lies without any remorse, skipping classes at school, and taking things that didn't belong to her. This resulted in petty clashes at home every now and then, with Shẹ̀wà being more forgiving than I was about her behaviour.

Despite the occasional tension, I found comfort in the strong bond between Jọlá and Shẹ̀wà. One day, I stumbled upon them sitting on the living room floor, exchanging inside jokes and laughing uncontrollably. It was a heart-warming sight, and I couldn't stop myself from smiling, grateful for the special connection they had built. Suddenly, Jọlá got up and walked over to me, plopping down on the couch next to me.

"AK, can I talk to you for a minute?" she asked, her voice hesitant.

"Sure, what's on your mind?" I responded, turning to face her.

"I just wanted to say sorry for lying to you and Shẹ̀wà. I know I messed up, but I promise I'll be better," Jọlá said, her eyes downcast.

Shẹ̀wà chimed in. "Jewels, we forgive you. This is gonna sound cliché, but honesty truly is the best policy. Withholding the truth or blatantly lying to us will always make us question your honesty. So, put your trust issues aside and trust us. You'd better come correct."

Jọlá nodded, a look of relief on her face. "I will. Thank you, Shẹ̀wà. You know you're like a mother to me, right? I appreciate you so much."

I watched as Shèwà eyes softened, while feeling deep admiration for the woman I had married. She had a motherly quality that evidently made everyone feel loved and cared for.

Then Jolá spoke up with enthusiasm. "Also, I've been thinking. I want to study child psychology. You know how little kids just love me, right? Well, it's the only job I can see myself being passionate about in the future. What do you both think?"

"That's fantastic! Understanding what makes little minds tick is an amazing career path," I said with pride.

"Just make sure you research the subjects and courses you need to become a child psychologist," Shèwà advised. "Jewels the psychologist. Has a nice ring to it," she teased.

"I'm already on it. Thank you," Jolá said with a smile.

As Jolá left the room, I squeezed Shèwà's hand and said, "You are truly a gem, babe. I don't know what I would do without you."

She smiled back at me. "I'm just doing what anyone would do in my position. Jolá is a part of our family, and we have to look out for her."

I leaned in and kissed her softly on the lips, feeling grateful for the blessing of having such a wonderful wife. As I looked at her, I reminisced about that night at the Christmas party, where our love story began. "Hey, do you remember that time we played charades?" I said, nudging her playfully.

"Of course, I do," she replied, laughing. "You were terrible at it!"

We both burst out laughing, and I was filled with gratitude for this woman who had stood by me through thick and thin. As we held hands, I was reminded that sometimes, the greatest love stories are the ones that start with a simple game of charades. I thought about how blessed I was to have her in my life, imagining Jọlá's mother looking down from heaven, smiling at the family she had left behind.

Chapter 13

I had always imagined, despite my upbringing, that marriage and family life could be just like the movies – you meet someone, fall in love, get married, have kids, and live happily ever after. Well, it only took a number of reality checks to realise that life is far more complicated than that. Life always comes at you fast with its curveballs.

One evening six months into our marriage, I savoured the taste of Shẹ̀wà's homemade meal of jollof rice and fried plantain while we sat at the dinner table. Suddenly, she announced that she had a surprise for me. "Cover your eyes," she instructed with a mischievous grin. As I obliged, I heard the rustling of plastic and the clattering of objects being arranged on the table. My heart raced in anticipation. Finally, Shẹ̀wà said, "Okay, open your eyes."

My eyes flew open, and I found myself staring at four plastic casings, their long, thin shapes almost beckoning me to pick them up. I realised what they were – pregnancy tests. My heart began to pound loudly in my chest. I was inundated with huge doses of disbelief, excitement, and panic all at once.

"Oh my gosh!" I exclaimed, my voice thick with emotion. "Is this real?" I found myself staring at Shẹ̀wà in awe, my mind struggling to process the news. "When did you find out?"

As I gazed at the positive results, my mind conjured up images of tiny fingers and toes, the soft coos of a newborn, and the scent of baby powder. A wave of gratitude swept me, as I thought about the new chapter that lay ahead for us. I was in awe of Shẹ̀wà, the incredible ability to bring life into the world, and the depth of our love for each other.

As the weeks passed by, our excitement for parenthood grew. We dreamed of painting the kid's room with vibrant colours and discussed names as we eagerly anticipated the arrival of our little one. The air was filled with pure joy and anticipation.

But then, everything changed in an instant. Our world was shattered when we lost the pregnancy at the eight-week mark. The pain was unbearable, and we felt blindsided by the sudden loss. I felt a weight on my chest that I couldn't shake. The same deep sadness I had experienced from losing loved ones before, but this time, it felt tenfold worse. As we drove home from the maternity care centre, on our way from confirming the miscarriage, the sorrow felt palpable. In my mind, I kept recollecting the scene of the ultrasound, with the image of the baby that wasn't there. The grief was all-consuming, as though I were drowning in it.

I gripped the steering wheel tightly as I navigated the Honda Civic down the familiar route back home. The air in the car was thick with silence, only interrupted by the occasional sound of Shẹ̀wà's soft weeping.

Suddenly, the shrill ringtone of Shẹ̀wà's phone shattered the stillness, and Jọlá's panicked voice filled the car.

"Shẹ̀wà… can you come get me please? I'm being attacked in front of school… Can you hear me? Come help me, please!" Jọlá's call was abrupt, and ended just as Shẹ̀wà was about ask for more details. Shẹ̀wà and I shared a quick glance. Without us uttering a word to each other, my instincts kicked in and I made a sharp U-turn, turning the car in the direction of Jọlá's school. I pressed my foot down hard on the gas pedal, feeling the powerful engine roar to life beneath me, the vibrations pulsing through the steering wheel as I swerved around the corner onto the road leading to Jọlá's school. I felt like I was on a race track; the acrid smells of burnt rubber and petrol filled my nostrils, and when I arrived at the school, the tyres screeched against the slick pavement. I caught a glimpse of several figures wearing balaclavas and dragging a struggling Jọlá by her braids, while other students stood by, holding their phones out, laughing and recording the clash without intervention.

Without hesitation, Shẹ̀wà bolted out of the car with a burst of adrenaline-fuelled strength, and she charged towards the bullies like a force of nature. Her movements were quick and calculated, and she struck each of them with lightning-fast open-palmed thuds to their chests, sending them flying and crashing to the ground; one even ended up in the nearby thorny bushes. Her stance was confident and unyielding, like an immovable pillar in the face of danger. All the other students flinched in fear. With the same strength and precision, she scooped up Jọlá, gripping her wrist tightly, and they made their escape. The other students stared in stupefied silence as Shẹ̀wà calmly got back into the Honda Civic, shut the door and called out, "Let's go!"

That was my cue. I drove off like I was in a getaway car. It all happened so fast, like we were never there, and there was a collective look of awe on everyone else's faces as they watched us drive off.

As we sped away from the scene of the attack, I stole a glance at Jọlá through the rear-view mirror. She was battered and bruised, but her eyes were filled with a fierce determination that I couldn't help but admire.

"What happened back there?" I asked, my voice laced with concern.

"It was some stupid bitch who—" Jọlá began to rant, and I interrupted her.

"Language, Jewels." I cautioned her crudeness.

Jọlá tried to cool off through gritted teeth, her words punctuated with anger and frustration. My protective instincts towards her grew as she recounted the events that led to the attack.

"It was a bully called Kirsty. She blamed me for snitching to the teachers about her, which led to her getting expelled this week. She also claimed I stole her boyfriend. Which is a big lie – I don't even really talk to the guy she was referring to," she explained.

"Do you know who the other girls in those masks were? Were they friends of hers?" Shẹ̀wà asked as she checked on Jọlá's wounds and awaited her answer.

"I don't know the other girls, but I could recognise Kirsty's voice when she spoke," Jọlá clarified.

"The moment we get home we need to call student services to report this. Maybe even the police." I paused, took a breath to change the tone of my voice from a concerned to a light-hearted one. "Maybe if you had taken those self-defence classes I signed you up for more seriously, you wouldn't have needed saving, huh?" I joked, trying to lighten the mood. But the air in the car remained heavy, and my attempt at humour fell flat.

As we drove, Shẹ̀wà and I exchanged worried glances. We both knew that this incident could not go unreported. We may have saved Jọlá from physical harm, but the emotional scars would take much longer to heal. When we approached home, I parked the car in the driveway and hoped we could find a way to move forward from that traumatic day as a family. We successfully got through to student services by phone call, and they promised to escalate the issue to the police. The teacher did mention, as a footnote to our call, that if Jọlá had attended her class which was ongoing at the same time, the altercation may have been deferred or avoided completely. As the call ended, I went to find Jọlá in the kitchen. Shẹ̀wà nursed Jọlá by dressing her wounds, while Jọlá held some ice to her head.

"Listen to me, Jewels, you need to understand that your education is important. You can't keep skipping classes and getting into fights. It's not going to end well for you. You need to focus on your studies and stay out of trouble as much as you can, whether or not it's your fault."

Jọlá just shrugged her shoulders and looked away. I knew that I wasn't getting through to her. I decided to take a different approach.

"Jewels, I know that things have been tough for you. But you need to understand that you can't keep running away from your problems. You need to face them head-on, and that means going to school and studying hard. I know that you're capable of doing great things, but you need to believe in yourself."

Jọlá looked at me, and for a moment, I thought I saw a hint of compliance in her eyes. She nodded her head and said, "I'll try."

"Jewels, I know that you've been going through a lot lately," I began, "and I want you to know that I'm here for you."

Jọlá looked up at me, her eyes red and puffy. "I don't know what's wrong with me, AK," she said. "I just feel so angry all the time, and I can't seem to focus in classes, which is probably why I walk out of them."

I took a deep breath, knowing that this was going to be a difficult conversation. Shèwà got up, having completed dressing the injuries. We shared a brief acknowledging glance at each other as she left the room. "Jewels, I think that maybe some of your behaviour is as a result of the trauma that you've experienced."

Jọlá's eyes widened in surprise. "What trauma?" she asked.

I hesitated for a moment, wondering if I was doing the right thing by bringing up the past. But then I remembered that Jọlá needed to confront her pain in order to move forward.

"You know what I'm talking about, Jewels," I said gently. "Your mother's death, and everything that led up to it. The domestic violence that you and your mother endured."

Jọlá's face crumpled, and she began to cry. "I... I miss her so much," she whispered. "And I hate myself for the way I treated her before she died. I knew she was sick, but I was selfish about it. I was rude to her, the last time you took me to go see her, because... because I assumed she intentionally chose not to come home in time for Christmas. Do you remember?" Jọlá, in the moment, triggered a memory that I had somehow repressed, and I had never made a connection or regarded the significance of the events she was highlighting.

The day she was referring to was the last day we had both seen Aunty Mimi alive.

Aunty Mimi had said she had to stay to do more tests in the hospital and wouldn't be able to make it home for Christmas. Which Jọlá misconstrued and assumed her mother had a choice in the matter. Jọlá suggested, "Why don't you come home, and do the tests after Christmas?"

Aunty clarified, "I'm sorry, baby girl. I couldn't, even if I wanted to."

This got Jọlá angry, throwing a tantrum and choosing not to hug her mother or say goodbye as we left the hospital. That was Jọlá's final memory of her mother.

I nodded as I recollected the memory, and put my arm around her, holding her close. "Jewels, it's okay to grieve," I said. "And it's okay to cry. But you need to forgive yourself, and your dad. You can't carry this pain around forever."

Jọlá nodded, wiping away her tears. "I know," she said. "But how do I do that?"

"You see, the reverberations of childhood trauma are likely to inform who we become as adults. Even with me, I know I have had to break the vicious cycle of my imperfect father figures by trying to become a better one myself. And thanks to you, I can add fatherhood to my portfolio of achievements… So, remember, your past should never dictate your future. That being said, I think we should talk to a therapist," I suggested. "Someone who can help you work through your emotions and find ways to heal."

Jọlá looked at me, her eyes hopeful. "Do you really think that will help?"

"I do," I said, giving her a reassuring smile. "And I'll be there for you every step of the way."

As we hugged, a soothing solace swathed us both. Jọlá still had a long way to go, but I knew that we would get through this together.

— ∞ —

It had been a few weeks since the ultrasound scan at the maternity care centre, where we received the devastating news of our miscarriage. The weight of that experience still lingered over us, casting a heavy grey cloud over our daily lives. Shẹ̀wà and I sat down together to talk about what we could do next on our journey towards having a child. As we spoke, Shẹ̀wà's face suddenly lit up with a beam of clarity.

"AK, I've been thinking," she said. "Maybe we should both get fertility checks."

I was surprised by her suggestion and raised my eyebrows. "Why?"

Shẹ̀wà shrugged. "Just to make sure that there isn't anything else we need to address. Plus, it might give us some peace of mind."

I nodded, seeing the wisdom in her words. We decided to move forward with the tests, and the results were a mixed bag. Shẹ̀wà's results came back quickly, and they were positive: her eggs were healthy with a normal count. In contrast, my histopathology infertility test results were not as encouraging. I was diagnosed with oligoasthenoteratozoospermia, a condition where my sperm count, motility, and shape were all below average. The new information hit me hard, like a heavy blow to my hopes and dreams. The news sent shockwaves through my body, leaving me feeling numb and helpless. I struggled to come to terms with the diagnosis, my mind reeling with questions and doubts. *How would this affect our chances of growing our family? Was there anything we could do to improve the situation?* Despite the uncertainty and fear that consumed me, I knew that I had to face the truth head-on and find a way forward. The report detailed the following:

Histopathology Infertility Test	Patient name: Akándé Jímọ̀h
Sample 21A00100494	Collected at 8:45 am
Test Time	9:05 am
Has entire sample ejaculated been collected?	Yes

Days since last ejaculation?	5
Is there a known risk of infection?	No
Spermatozoa concentration	3.6 million/ml
Total sperm concentration	17.6 million
Progressive (movement)	6%
Non-progressive (movement)	2%
Immobile (movement)	92%
Normal morphology	0%
Abnormal morphology	100%
Head defects	100%
Mid-Piece defects	23%
Tail defects	9%
Colour	Normal
Volume	4.9ml
pH	7.5
Viscosity	Normal
Comments	Oligoasthenoteratozoospermia (OAT) – Concentration of spermatozoa and percentages of both progressively motile (PR) and morphologically normal spermatozoa are below the lower reference limits. End of Report

My heart felt heavy as I sat with Shẹ̀wà, going over the result and contemplating our next steps. The memory of our previous miscarriage was still fresh in my mind, a haunting grey cloud that refused to lift. But as we explored the possibility of intracytoplasmic sperm injection (ICSI), a specialised form of in vitro fertilisation, hope began to seep back into my soul. We met with fertility specialists, underwent medical and psychological evaluations, and ordered the necessary medications, all in the hopes of bringing a new life into this world.

Just as we were about to embark on the journey of ICSI, which involved sample collections, taking vitamins, medications, and injections, Shèwà surprised me with the news of yet another pregnancy. My heart skipped a beat as an eruption of excitement and fear overcame me. *What if we lose this baby too? What if something goes wrong?* But I refused to let those thoughts consume me. I focused on the present moment, relishing the joy of this precious news.

As the days passed, we reached the eight-week gestation mark – the same age at which we'd lost our previous baby. It was a nerve-wracking time, but as we crossed the threshold of the first trimester, we welcomed the miraculous milestone. Shèwà and I spent hours talking about birth plans, discussing pregnancy eating habits, and debating which colours to paint the baby's room. It felt surreal to be here again, a bit like a déjà vu, but this time felt different, more special.

We even had a secret system of sharing notes with each other, little details about what we hoped for our baby, a pool of potential baby names, the baby essentials, and our budget. These notes were our way of expressing the hope we had for our little one and distracting ourselves from the grief we had been experiencing. Even Jọlá was excited about the arrival of the little one. This was our divine intervention, a worthy testimony that we could not wait to share with the world. We were all excited for the forthcoming chapter in our lives, full of hope, anticipation, and love.

Chapter 14

Exhausted from a gruelling day at work, I stumbled through the door of my quiet living room and collapsed onto the plush couch. The weight of the day's stress and fatigue bore down on me, but I couldn't shake the nagging prompts and pinging notifications from my phone, signalling my storage capacity limit being reached. I proceeded to delete things from my phone like spam emails, duplicate pictures, redundant apps, and some text messages. But then I froze on one message that said "See you Christmas" with a heart emoji next to it. It was the last message from Aunty Mimi that lingered on my phone. Several years had gone by now since her untimely demise, but rereading the message made me realise I had finally transitioned into the acceptance stage of grieving. I missed her, maybe not as much as my mother, Dámi, or Jọlá did, but I missed her all the same.

Lost in my thoughts, I didn't notice Jọlá's presence until she was already in the room. Her shoulders were slumped, and her face etched with sorrow. I braced myself for a conversation, thinking it was going to be something academic or trivial, but her words left me a bit dazed.

"AK, do you ever think about forgiveness?" Her voice was barely above a whisper, but her question was deafening.

I looked at her, sensing the pain she carried in her heart. "What do you mean, Jewels?" I asked softly.

"I mean, do you think it's possible to forgive someone who has hurt you so deeply? Someone like my dad?" she murmured, her voice trembling with emotion.

I took a deep breath. Clearly this was a topic lingering on her mind – an idea I probably incepted in her thoughts from our earlier conversations. Despite our legal battles, I had no personal grudge towards Uncle Taj. But I knew that Jọlá had once looked up to her father like a hero, until he failed her. Her question hung heavy in the air, and I knew that there were no easy answers.

"Jewels, I don't think forgiveness is easy. But I do believe that it's necessary if you want to move on and heal."

Jọlá nodded slowly, looking lost in thought. I wondered if my response had been sufficient, and if she would ever be able to forgive her father for the abuse that she and her mother had suffered at his hands.

Later that day, I received a call from Dámi, who was ecstatic to tell me that her visa application had finally been approved. "I'm coming to London, you know!" she exclaimed over the phone.

A flurry of happiness for my cousin rattled within me, while simultaneously, a twinge of sadness emerged due to the reason for her visit. "We'll be glad to have you here, Dámi," I said to her. Forgiveness between Dámi and her dad was something of a hot topic too. Dámi had always blamed her father for not being able to travel to the UK. He had tried to get her into the country, but by fraudulent methods – which had caused many a quarrel between him and Aunty Mimi – therefore impeding Dámi's travel application process to the UK to see Jọlá or her mother. She had never been to the UK prior to this.

A few days later, my mother called me with the news that she and Dámi would be arriving in London in a few weeks, just in time for Aunty Mimi's birthday. She would've been forty years old. "We want to celebrate her life and remember the good times," Mum said. We never went to the cemetery on Christmas Day, as I always believed it important to celebrate the day of entry into this world, rather than the day of one's exit.

I was touched by my mother's words and promised to make sure that everything was ready for their arrival. In addition to the recently furnished baby's room, we had another guest room and could accommodate our guests.

When I told Jọlá and my wife, Shẹ̀wà, the news, they both smiled in excitement. "This is going to be a great reunion," Shẹ̀wà said, rubbing her growing belly.

That said, Jọlá looked hesitant. "What about my dad?" she asked. "Shouldn't we invite him too?"

I was a little surprised by Jọlá's suggestion, but I could see the determination in her eyes. "Are you sure, Jọlá?" I asked.

Jọlá nodded, her gaze unwavering. "I think it's time for us to start healing, AK. And forgiveness might be the first step."

Pure admiration bubbled up within me. I couldn't believe this child was speaking with such wisdom. I knew that this was not an easy decision for Jọlá to make, but I was grateful that she was willing to take the first step towards reconciliation. Aunty Mimi would want her daughter to be forgiving, but cautious. Her father could still be quite conniving. "Let's do it then," I said, smiling back at her. "We'll invite him to visit the cemetery with us on your mum's birthday."

As their cousin, I have had the opportunity to observe the lives of Dámi and Jọlá, the two sisters living in different cities. Dámi, the older sister, resides in Lagos, a bustling city that thrives, albeit with frequent corruption, classism, and oppression. On the other hand, Jọlá, the younger sister, lives in

London, a city that prides itself on being a melting pot of ethnicities and opportunities, possibly as an aftershock of Great Britain siphoning resources from its "commonwealth" colonies over the centuries.

Lagos and London are two cities with vastly different histories, but with many overlaps when it comes to classism, oppression, corruption, poverty gaps, and colonialism. As someone who has lived in both cities, I have experienced first-hand how these issues can impact individuals living in each place. In one city, I may be referred to as a Black person or a minority, whilst in the other city, I'm just referred to as a person, because I am part of the majority.

One of the most striking differences between Lagos and London is the blatant display of disparity between wealth and poverty. In Lagos, it is not uncommon to see luxury cars driving past run-down neighbourhoods where people live in extreme poverty. The wealthy live lavish lifestyles, while the poorer majority live in overcrowded and dilapidated homes, clamouring for electricity and clean water. In contrast, London's poverty is more hidden, but no less pervasive. The bitter sting of poverty can be felt in the lively streets of both Lagos and London, where the harsh reality of homelessness haunts the most vulnerable members of society. In Lagos, some poor families huddle together in shacks made of rusted metal sheets, live close to piles of refuse, or sleep under highway bridges. While in London, the dispossessed sleep rough in the cold concrete corners of the city's underbelly, even worse at sub-zero temperatures, where the frostbite of the winter season makes it near impossible to survive sleeping in the streets. Yet, despite the universality of poverty, the ways in which it presents itself in these two cities are vastly different.

In Lagos, the oppressive heat beats down on the tired and homeless, who, in extreme cases, rummage through garbage bins in search of scraps to feed their families. The stench of open sewers and overflowing waste piles fills the air, and the noise of honking horns and shouting vendors is a constant background hum. In contrast, London's poverty is more insidious, hiding in plain sight behind closed doors of cramped and overcrowded council flats, with some people surviving on government benefit schemes. The streets are cleaner, but the poverty gap is still massive, with the wealthy living in gated communities and the poor pushed to the margins.

Despite the differences, the effects of poverty are similar in both cities. Families are torn apart, children go hungry, and hopelessness seeps into every corner of life. Furthermore, the cycle of poverty is perpetuated by corrupt and institutionalised systems, both old and new, that leave the most vulnerable at the mercy of those in power. The impact of these structures is felt by individuals living in both Lagos and London, as they struggle to survive in a world that seems to have left them behind.

Interpretations of poverty may differ, but the experience of it is universal. One can only hope to bridge the gap between the haves and the have-nots, and create a world where everyone has the opportunity to thrive, irrespective of being in Lagos, London, or anywhere else in the world.

Another key difference between the two cities is their history of colonialism. London's history as a colonial power has left a legacy of systemic racism and inequality that is still present in many aspects of British society, with the vestiges of imperialism rippling across its Commonwealth associations to this day. Lagos, and the entirety of Nigeria as a colonial victim, on the other hand, was colonised by the British and then gained independence in 1960, but the country still struggles with the after-effects of colonialism. The corruption and oppression that Nigeria has been so infamous for were, to a great extent, introduced as a result of Nigeria's colonial subjugation and continue to plague the country's government and institutions today. The colonial rule of the past has also had a lasting impact on London's society, with the continued marginalisation of people of ethnic minorities and immigrants inadvertently leading to institutionalised racism and xenophobia.

Classism is a common issue in both cities, but the nature of it differs. In Lagos, classism is often based on wealth, nepotism, or "who you know", political affiliations, the car you own, the neighbourhood you live in, etcetera. In London, it can be based on education, bias, inherited privilege, access to resources, income, occupation and so on. Regardless of the specifics, classism can have a profound impact on the opportunities available to individuals in each city. With education, for instance, even those who can afford a university education in Nigeria still find it hard to get a job when they graduate. Meanwhile, in the UK there are graduate programmes in addition to student loan systems and scholarships that encourage university applications. This in turn leads to the long queues at the embassies and consulates of aspiring emigrants with a strong desire to leave Nigeria for the UK, seeking out better opportunities abroad.

The weight of oppression hangs heavily in both Lagos and London, seeping through every aspect of society. In Lagos, but maybe more so in other parts of Nigeria, there is still an undertone of tribalism, and marginalised groups struggle to break through the thick layers of prejudice that suffocate unity, making it challenging to flourish in a world that doesn't see that we are stronger together and weaker divided. In London, discrimination is a pervasive issue that gnaws at the foundations of society, chewing away at the dignity of minority ethnicities. Despite living in a city that is supposed to represent progress and multiculturalism, they are forced to navigate a world that constantly reminds them of their "otherness". The sharp edges of discrimination cut deep, slicing away at opportunities and experiences that should be accessible to all.

Despite the many challenges facing both cities, individuals in each place have found ways to resist oppression and strive for change. In Lagos, activists and organisations are working to combat corruption and promote human rights, while in London, some grassroots movements are fighting for racial and economic justice. Despite the shackles of the past, the people of Lagos and London persist. They carry with them their talents, enthusiasm, positivity, and kindness, always looking for ways to innovate and improve their lives. Taking a brisk walk through a place like Oshodi in Lagos, you see the vibrant colours of clothing and smell the spicy aromas of street food filling the air, a testament to the people's indomitable spirit. Taking a casual stroll along the roads of Camden Town in London, you would be privy to the sounds of different languages and the scent of multicultural cuisine wafting through the streets, a reminder of the city's diversity.

No matter the obstacles they face, the people of both cities remain optimistic, refusing to let the weight of their society's past drag them down. They continue to press forward, looking towards a brighter future. And personally, the experience of living in both England and Nigeria has expanded my horizons well beyond my comfort zone, especially in terms of acclimatising to cultural differences.

The sisters, Dámi and Jọlá, had grown up in vastly different environments. In Lagos, Dámi had to navigate a society where classism and tradition often intersected. As the older sister, she would normally have to be addressed with respect by her younger sister, who could never just call her by her name, even with a three-year age gap. In some cases, you would need to enforce a respectful prefix like "Sis" or "Big Sis". This is a way of acknowledging the older sister's higher position in the family hierarchy and showing deference to her. A kind of "seniority" if you will. Similarly, people who are not related by family ties are often addressed as "Uncle" or "Aunty" as a sign of respect for their age and position in society. This emphasis on respect for elders is not unique to Lagos but is a common feature of many cultures around the world. In some cultures, there are specific rituals or gestures that are used to show respect, such as bowing, prostrating, curtsying or kneeling. The concept of respect in Nigeria is closely tied to the idea of hierarchy and age. It is considered important to show respect to elders, whether they are family members or not, and this is typically done through the use of respectful titles and prefixes. But In London, Jọlá was free to call most people by their first names, without any scrutiny or enforcement of traditional respect. I'm her adoptive father, and she still refers to me as AK, which is fine by me.

The nature vs. nurture debate comes to mind when I consider the sisters' relationship. Despite growing up in different cities, their shared trauma of losing their mother should have brought them closer together. All the same, Jọlá's carefree adolescent phase and lack of effort in maintaining a relationship with her sister may have been influenced by her environment. In contrast, Dámi, who consistently reached out to her sister despite Jọlá's lack of response, may have been influenced by her upbringing in a society that values strong family bonds and has a custom for offering guidance.

Obviously, nurture highlights the impact an environment and upbringing can have on an individual's mindset and behaviour. The contrasting atmospheres of Lagos and London may have influenced the sisters' relationship and their individual attitudes towards tradition and family. Despite the distance between them, the technology of mobile phones should have allowed them to communicate instantly, yet it was their differing mindsets that kept them apart. So, I had hoped that having them under the same roof over the ensuing weeks would result in their relationship growing beyond mere trauma-bonding, evolving into one of solidarity and empathy as they coped with the loss of their mother and the grief caused by their father.

I sat behind the wheel of the Honda Civic, eagerly waiting for my mother and Dámi to arrive at Heathrow Airport. Shèwà sat in the passenger side next to me, her pregnant belly causing her seatbelt to be a bit tighter than usual. I could feel her excitement, and it was contagious.

Finally, I saw them walking towards the car. Dámi's eyes widened when she saw Shèwà's baby bump, and my mother couldn't hide her grin either.

"Oh, my goodness, look at you, Shèwà!" my mum exclaimed as she approached the car. "You're glowing!"

Shèwà chuckled. "Thank you, Mama B." My mother had insisted from the very first time she met Shèwà that she be referred to as Mama B. "It's good to see you. How was the flight?"

Dámi interjected and leaned in for a hug. "It was good, you know, just glad I can stretch my legs now."

As I pulled out of the airport, Dámi peppered Shèwà with questions about the pregnancy, and my mum listened intently. I smiled to myself, grateful for the warmth that filled the car.

Jọlá was waiting for us at home. As soon as she saw her sister, she hugged her tightly, tears streaming down her face. A far cry from her stoic and inexpressive demeanour years ago at her mother's funeral. Mum held both girls close, and they all stood there for a moment, lost in each other's embrace.

My mother and Shẹ̀wà wasted no time making plans to head to Dalston market, to purchase necessary ingredients in order to create an array of Nigerian delicacies. The very next day, we all set out on a food shopping trip. As we strolled down the aisles, the vibrant colours of the vegetables and fruits caught our eyes. The bright green okra, the deep red tomatoes, and the yellow plantains all looked so fresh and inviting. My cousins eagerly picked up the food items, feeling their textures and inhaling their fragrances.

Back at home, my mother and cousins took over the kitchen. The sounds of chopping, sizzling, and stirring filled the house. They encouraged Shẹ̀wà to relax so as not to overexert herself. I wasn't even in the kitchen, but the smell of onions frying in oil wafted through the air, and my mouth started to water in anticipation. I could hear the clinking of pots and pans, the hissing of spices being added to the pot, and the crackling of meat as it seared in the pan.

As I sat in the living room, I was transported back to my childhood days spent in Lagos with my grandma. I could picture her in the kitchen, with the same sounds and smells filling the air. The feeling of nostalgia overwhelmed me, swaddling me in a blanket of comfort and warmth.

Finally, it was time to eat, and my mother and cousins presented a feast fit for royalty. The table was adorned with jollof rice, coconut rice, fried plantains, ẹgusi soup, pounded yam, and a variety of meat dishes. As I took my first bite, I was hit with an explosion of flavours, each one more delicious than the last. The sensation of the soft and fluffy pounded yam, paired with the rich and tasty ẹgusi soup, was a delight to my taste buds.

While we ate, we shared stories and memories, which filled me with gratitude for the cherished moment with my family. The entire atmosphere brought back memories of my childhood, and I realised how much I missed those days spent with my grandma.

During dinner, Jọlá asked, "Mummy, for my mum's anniversary, what do you think about me asking my dad to come and pay his respects too?"

My mother's face tightened. "I don't know, Jọlá. It's been so long since we've seen him."

Dámi spoke up. "I think it would be good for us to forgive him, Mummy. We can't hold on to the past forever, you know."

My mother sighed. "I know you're right, Dámi. I'll think about it."

A few days later, Jọlá called her father to invite him to the anniversary. He was initially dismissive and ended the conversation, but called back later to say he would keep his calendar open. Jọlá was cautiously optimistic, but my mum was less than pleased.

"He's just doing it to save face," she muttered to me. "I don't trust him one bit." My mum went into a mellow tirade about his corrupt nature, his false accusations of female genital mutilations against her, and his decade-long empty promises of paying for Dámi's education. My mum was bitter, and still blamed him for her sister's death.

I put my arm around her shoulder. "In the immortal words of Desmond Tutu, 'without forgiveness, there's no future.' Forgiveness is important, Mum. Let's focus on that."

I suddenly remembered something I had wanted to ask my mother. "Oh, and speaking of forgiveness, when it came to Grandpa, your dad, were you ever able to forgive him for the spiteful way he addressed you, Grandma, and everyone else in his will?"

"Oh, I hold no ill will towards my father. The will did not surprise me. I had known the man all my life, and I had always known he was capable of doing such a thing. It was just so unfortunate your grandma died so soon after he did," my mother said, her expression matching the peace of mind her words conveyed.

"And did they ever build that arthritis charity foundation in Grandpa's name?" I asked.

"Huh? What foundation?" she asked sarcastically. "We never saw one brick laid towards that foundation. Those will-executor lawyers absconded with everything."

"Everything?" I sought to clarify.

"Yes, everything!" she said emphatically. "From the bank accounts, the properties, the bonds... everything."

"Wow, even the walking sticks?" I asked jokily.

"Mscheww..." She sucked her teeth and giggled. "Even your grandpa's precious walking sticks, all gone. The only thing that was left, which was stipulated in the will, was the family house. It was rented out for a long while, because there was no way all my father's mistresses and daughters could live in there amicably. So, recently myself and the rest of my half-sisters met and decided to sell it. We plan to split the proceeds equally amongst ourselves."

I let out a gasp, taking in all of the new information from my mother, while trying to come to terms with my childhood home being sold off.

"I had so many memories there. In fact, all my childhood memories were created there," I said with an uncontrollably saddened feeling.

"I know. Mine too."

— ∞ —

On the day of the anniversary, I drove us to the cemetery. We were all chatty in the car on the way there, and we soon found an ideal parking spot not far from Aunty Mimi's gravestone. My mum remained silent when Uncle Taj arrived and parked his eye-catching Toyota RAV4 close to our car, dwarfing our Honda Civic in comparison. Everyone else greeted him politely, except my mother. As we walked towards the gravesite, the awkward tension was palpable.

My mother kept her distance from Uncle Taj, and the rest of the group made small talk. Finally, we reached the grave, and everyone stood in silence for a moment, then proceeded to share whispered moments of affection with Aunty Mimi. Just a few metres away, there was a funeral service going on, with the noise from the ceremony quite audible. We could see a group of about thirty people, mostly young teens, all dressed in black, mourning the death of another teenager. There was a huge portrait picture of the deceased, and he looked about the same age as Jọlá. Their ceremony looked quite flamboyant. But suddenly, a loud noise interrupted our sombre moment, as chaos visibly ensued when three boys in masks appeared, brandishing guns and knives.

Everyone was screaming and crying. Some froze, unsure of what to do. My protective instincts kicked in, and I grabbed Shẹ̀wà and my mother, pulling them behind a nearby tombstone, waiting for the perfect time to run for the car. The assailants started shooting, loud gunshots all over the place, as everyone ran for cover. Uncle Taj guided his daughters to safety. As we began running towards the car, I saw a few people fall towards the ground, some getting shot, others just falling in the stampede. Then, in the blink of an eye, I felt a sharp, incredible pain in my back. I looked down to see blood gushing from my side. Some of the blood smeared over Shẹ̀wà's baby bump.

"AK, are you okay? Babe!" Shẹ̀wà said in a shrieking voice.

"Don't worry about it, my love. Let's just get to the car," I responded, trying my best to be brave.

I continued to run, ignoring the pain, but then I stumbled and fell to the ground. As I lay there, I could hear the assailants continuing to shoot, but everything else became inaudible. Everyone screamed in concern and disbelief, with Uncle Taj, who was way ahead of me with Jọlá and Dámi, rushing back to carry me as I lost control of all motor functions, lying on the ground, eyes to the sky.

"Come on, Akándé, we have to get you out of here," Uncle Taj yelled as he carried my limp body.

I could feel the blood soaking through my shirt, my body swaying back and forth as I struggled to keep my eyes open. The pain was unbearable, and I could feel my life slipping away. Uncle Taj's face was the last thing I saw before I lost consciousness.

"Stay with me, Akándé, stay with me," Uncle Taj said, his voice trembling with concern.

As I drifted off into unconsciousness, a sudden fear came over me – that I might never see my family again.

Act V: Continuum

"Father's life teeters,
Memories rush, hopes in haze,
Unborn child's embrace."
- Tòbí

Chapter 15

I was seated at the back of a rickshaw, my eyes meeting the sight of the driver in the rear-view mirror. His rose-tinted horn-rimmed glasses obstructed his eyes, and his shirt was a burst of colour, beckoning the eye to linger and admire its playful patterns. I tried to decipher the miniature animal-like details on his shirt, but before I could, he stammered out with a toothpick in his mouth, "Here's yo-yo-your stop. The Zion Plaza building is just th-th-that way."

"Thank you," I said, hopping out of the rickshaw into a busy marketplace. As I kept walking, I suddenly approached a skyscraper building. At the reception, I mentioned who I was and what I was there to do. I passed the security checks and was given a visitor ID to proceed to the lift. My interview would be on the fifth floor. I stepped out of the lift, and I was filled with a mix of nervousness and excitement that I couldn't fight off. A lady with a clipboard in hand greeted me as I took my first few steps out of the lift. She introduced herself as Miss Dorothy and asked me to follow her to a conference room. I couldn't avoid hearing the clacking sound of her three-inch heels on the marble floor. The open-plan office space was empty, and she and I could have been the only ones on the entire floor. We entered a conference room, and she began to explain the interview steps to me.

"This interview will be divided into three stages: an oral interview, a written test, and a hands-on practical assessment. Only one of these stages will be timed. The other two will depend on your performance, which basically means they could end quickly or could keep going for as long as necessary. Any guesses as to which one is timed?"

I responded with uncertainty, "Err, the hands-on one?"

"Hmm, okay, if you say so. I won't confirm that just yet because me giving you any clues is practically cheating. Do you have any questions before we start? Oh, and by the way, do you have a printed copy of your CV?"

As I was about to answer, a security guard interrupted us, saying, "There is someone at the reception here to see you, sir."

"You go ahead. When you're back, we will start with the oral interview, and then proceed with the others afterwards."

I followed the security officer back down to the ground floor. As I walked towards the reception, my eyes were drawn to the unmistakable shirt adorned with drawings of wildlife on the man standing just ahead. To my surprise, I realised it was the rickshaw driver, his toothpick still lodged in his mouth, but this time, he held my CV in his hand.

"You found me just in time," I said, happy to see a familiar face.

"You-you-you dropped this in my cab, so-so-so I tho-tho-thought I would bring it back fo-fo-fo-fo-for you," he said, speaking in a familiar accent, pointing my CV back at me. Beyond merely being my rickshaw driver, it was as if I knew him – perhaps from another time or another place – but I couldn't pinpoint it. As I retrieved my CV from him, I intended to engage in small talk, but the man just walked off, waved, and shouted, "Goo-goo-good luck!"

"Thank you!" I shouted back at him, and he waved back in acknowledgement. I made my way back to the lift, showing my visitor card to the security guard, who nodded and gestured me back to the lift.

Back upstairs, the lights over the desk spaces in the distance started to flicker in an ominous manner, something I hadn't noticed earlier. Past the open-plan areas, I walked into the conference room, presenting my CV to the interviewer, who was drinking from a glass cup. I caught sight of a blender in the corner.

"Would you like a smoothie?" she offered.

"What's in it?" I asked.

"Just vegetables. You know, carrots, cabbage, and kale. It's been said the smoothie combination keeps you looking and feeling younger," she answered.

"No thank you," I responded politely.

I sat nervously in front of her, my palms sweaty and my heart racing. I had no idea what job I was being interviewed for, but the lady just kept saying I came highly recommended. So, I played along like I knew what I was getting myself into. I pondered what kind of job required an oral interview, a written interview, and a practical interview. The interviewer began to explain the interview process to me. I tried my best to listen, but my mind kept wandering. I wondered if my casual blue jeans and beige cotton t-shirt met the appropriate dressing standards for the interview, if my CV was impressive enough, and if I was going to be able to answer all of the interviewer's questions.

As the interviewer started the oral interview, I took a deep breath and tried to focus. She asked me about my job experience and my aspirations, and I answered as honestly as I could. Despite my attempts to project sophistication, confidence, and knowledge, I couldn't shake the nagging feeling of being slightly out of my depth.

When the interviewer asked where I hoped to see myself in five years, I hesitated. I didn't seem to have a clear plan for my future, and I didn't want to sound like I was just winging it. I took a moment to collect my thoughts before answering with vague optimism. After a few more questions, the interviewer asked if I had any questions for her. I paused for a moment before asking for feedback on how she thought the interview was going. I wanted to make sure I wasn't making any major mistakes that could cost me the job.

The interviewer respectfully declined, saying, "It's too early in the process to give you any feedback, I'm afraid."

I nodded, feeling a little disappointed but also relieved.

Next came the written interview. The interviewer handed me a sheet of paper and turned it face down in front of me.

"Look over there – that stop-clock will start at exactly sixty seconds, counting down to zero. Start when I say so. Stop when I say so. You have one minute. Please follow my instructions."

I spotted the stop-clock, immediately assuming this was a speed and accuracy test.

"Start!"

As the interviewer instructed me to flip over the sheet of paper and start the test, a heavy weight settled in the pit of my stomach. A torrent of dread inundated me. I had never been good at timed tests, and the thought of having to answer twenty brain-teaser and mathematical questions in just one minute made me feel queasy.

I quickly realised that the questions were not what I expected, and I panicked.

50 seconds left.

Question (1)

Using only addition, add eight 8s to get the number 1,000.

My answer: 8+8+8+88+888 = 1000

If you were running a race and passed the person in 2nd place, what position would you be in now?

My answer: Second place

Two questions down, eighteen to go. I stole a glance at the stop-clock...

35 seconds left.

Something drew my attention to the instructions at the top of the page, which I'd missed at the start:

Follow these instructions. Do not answer any of the questions listed from 1 to 20. You are to submit your notepad with nothing written in it. Good luck!

30 seconds left.

I had clearly wasted precious time on the first two questions. I looked up at the stop-clock.

I knew I had to act fast if I wanted to salvage the situation. I quickly crossed off everything I had written on the page, ripped it out of the notepad, crumpled it up, and tossed it into the bin in the corner of the room.

20 seconds left.

The interviewer raised an eyebrow and gave me a sceptical look. The final few seconds felt like forever. Then the stop-clock beeped.

0 seconds left.

"Stop!"

"Finished," I said, trying a little too hard to sound confident.

"I saw what you did there, but I'll allow it," she said with a hint of irritation. "How did you find the test?"

I swallowed hard, hoping I hadn't screwed up the interview or chances of moving to the next stage. "I got to understand the instructions a little late," I said, trying to sound apologetic. "But the instructions do say I have to present a blank notepad to you. Hence why I, err... rectified my mistake mid-test."

The interviewer nodded slowly and scribbled something on her clipboard. I couldn't tell if it was a good or bad sign. I just hoped that I hadn't made a complete fool of myself in front of her.

"It's time for the final stage of the interview," Miss Dorothy said, standing and holding the conference room door for me to exit.

I took a deep breath as I stepped out of the conference room and into the expansive open-plan office space. The flickering neon lights above the endless rows of computer desks made me feel uneasy. The office was anything but a buzzing hive of activity. The interviewer led me to a solitary workstation, and I couldn't escape the eerie feeling of isolation, like we two were the only ones on the entire floor of the building. She pulled out a chair for me.

"Here you go. Sit here," Miss Dorothy said in a gentle voice.

"Okay," I replied, with nervousness rising within me.

"I won't ask if you have any questions, that is part of the mystique of the test. All the best," she added before walking off.

I took a deep breath and looked at the screen in front of me, which displayed a cryptic-looking riddle.

WHAT IS IN THE ROOM, AND NEVER FORGETS?

There was a text field, with a blinking cursor waiting for me to input my answer. I began typing in an answer impatiently, hoping to get it right on my first attempt. But as soon as I pressed the submit button, the computer responded with "Incorrect answer!" I let out a sigh, frustrated with myself for jumping the gun.

Why did I type in "Air"? Of course, it's in every room, but it obviously has no memory to even forget.

The screen went dark, and I saw my reflection staring back at me. Suddenly, a prompt came up: "Two attempts left." My heart raced as the riddle came back up on the screen in bold text.

WHAT IS IN THE ROOM, AND NEVER FORGETS?

The lights' flickering intensified. I began to panic, racking my brain for an answer. But then I remembered the shirt of the rickshaw driver who'd brought me to the interview. The colourful shirt was filled with small illustrations of wildlife, including antelopes, giraffes, elephants, lions, and hyenas.

"In the room? Never forgets?" I whispered to myself, feeling a spark of inspiration. "Antelopes, giraffes, elephants, lions… Elephants! An elephant in the room. An elephant never forgets."

With newfound self-assurance, I typed in my answer and pressed submit. Suddenly, the screen erupted into a congratulatory fanfare, with digital ribbons flying on-screen all over my response.

But as I basked in the glory of my victory, I began to realise that there was more to this interview than met the eye. I'd gained access to the computer's mainframe, and I realised that the interview had only just begun…

As I sat in front of my computer screen, the artificial glow of the fluorescent tubes in the ceiling cast a sickly hue around the room, and my attention was drawn to the flickering. The constant dance of light had been a distraction at first, but now, as the flickering began to subside, I found myself strangely comforted by its presence. Though it didn't stop outright, the soft pulses of light had become a steady background rhythm, lulling me into tranquillity as I focused on the task at hand. On the screen, there were these three folders glaring right back at me, named RED, AMBER, and GREEN. Moving the mouse cursor to hover over each folder, I got more information:

RED (3,811 files)
AMBER (11,006 files)
GREEN (7,110 files)

I clicked on the AMBER folder, observing that it contained numerous video files. Each video looked to be titled by a date/time stamp. I selected one of the videos, and as it began to load, I saw at the bottom of the video three options:

(1) Relive Memory.
(2) Valuable lesson?
(3) End Session.

I clicked on "Relive Memory", but a prompt appeared, saying "Please put glasses and headphones on". Confused, I looked around, but I couldn't find any glasses. Instinctively, I used my fingertips to feel the underside of the workstation table and found something that fit the description of glasses. I pulled them out and noticed that they had a cable that led from the frame of the glasses to the bottom of the computer. Next to the glasses, I found a sophisticated set of headphones, which I put over my head. I also put the glasses over my eyes, and I already felt like I was having an immersive experience without even playing the video yet.

As I pressed play, it immediately felt like I was sucked into the video. It was akin to virtual reality – like reliving a past experience, but viewing it from a first-person perspective. In real time, I was being taunted and bullied by kids in school uniform. It was a day in boarding school, I must've been about fourteen years old. There was one big-looking sixteen-year-old standing right in front of me. I remembered this moment; the older boy was in the middle of extorting me, but I had, just in time, hidden the bottle of fruit juice he wanted from me.

"Where did you put the bottle?" the older boy asked.

"I don't know."

"Well, I'm going to help you remember. I'm going to help you flashback."

As the older boy said this, I knew he didn't mean a literal flashback; he instead intended to jog my memory via hot slaps. The other kids egged him on for this highly anticipated slap. His palms were wide, his arms outstretched at each side mimicking the crucifix, and gradually motioning towards me. He froze for a moment, as I stared at him staring at me.

"Is that your final answer?" the older boy asked.

I don't kn—"

Before I could finish my sentence, all I could hear was ringing in my ears. The older boy had slapped me with so much force from both sides that I was unable to turn either cheek sideways. I just stood there as the vibrations reverberated through my body.

"How about now? Do you remember?" the older boy asked.

"Yes, yes, I do!" I responded with tears streaming down my face, hands covering my face as I felt the soreness, exacerbated by how quickly my cheeks began to swell.

And just like that, I was out of the video. The options came back up:

(1) Relive Memory.

(2) Valuable lesson?

(3) End Session.

What valuable lesson can I possibly learn from that? I was violated, and my emotions felt raw. I chose the "Valuable lesson?" option. More options came up.

Select option: YES, MAYBE, or NO.

I chose the "NO" option, and immediately a dialog box came up underneath my selection with a "WHY?"

I typed on the keyboard, "Because I was a victim, and those bullies were idiots", then I clicked on the submit button. Right afterwards, the video file moved from the AMBER folder to the RED folder automatically, and the computer gave a beeping notification as the number of files in the folders changed. AMBER lost a file; RED gained one.

RED (3,812 files)
AMBER (11,005 files)
GREEN (7,110 files)

I navigated to the RED folder, scanning its contents until my gaze fell upon the same video file I had just watched, now accompanied by my new commentary. It had obviously moved from the AMBER folder, and I wondered what prompted the software to do so. Perhaps it was my response? My fingers traced a path to the GREEN folder. I adjusted my designated glasses and slid them onto the bridge of my nose. With a deep breath, I pressed play on a new video.

The video transported me to a restaurant, where I was with a female friend from years ago. I was reminded of the intricate details of this encounter. I could hear her voice. I could see the pained expression etched across her face as she posed a question that she had asked me several times before. "So, what are we?"

I was dumbfounded. She was a single mother raising a seven-year-old child, and I had selfishly approached her for advice, for insight on how to navigate the path of parenthood alone, given that we shared this commonality. It had escalated to a point of intimacy and complicated things, especially since she knew Jǫlá, and I knew her son.

"You flirt with other girls, even when I'm present," she accused. "It's as though you have no regard for me or us."

She had been my support, my rock through thick and thin. When I was low on funds, she'd provided me with groceries, gifts, and I got all the perks of a relationship without me giving back any assurance of commitment. She'd even served as a character witness to the social workers, which aided me in gaining special guardianship rights to Jǫlá. Persistently, she asked again, "So, what are we?"

"I'm not seeing anyone else, if that's what you're worried about," I tried to assure her, but I realised that I couldn't alter the narrative of this memory.

I could see the tears rolling down her cheeks as she cried, "I just feel like if you're not going to man up, then what are we doing here?"

As I reached out to comfort her, the video ended, just under a minute long.

I chose the "Valuable lesson?" option. More options came up.

This time, I chose the "YES" option, and immediately a dialog box came up underneath my selection with a "WHY?"

To my surprise, the dialog box already had my opinions pre-populated in the text box. It read: "Despite my love for her personality, I couldn't explain why I wasn't happy or eager to pursue a relationship with her. I was thankful for all she had done, but I didn't want to continue taking advantage of her kindness at the expense of my happiness."

So, I didn't alter the comment in the dialog box, but I added, "I hope she finds the happiness I couldn't provide for her." I hit save and closed the video. The file glowed green, a beacon of the video staying put in its rightful home, the GREEN folder.

I had a theory about the logic behind the files, folders, and comments. I hoped my next action would prove me right. Adjusting my headphones, I eagerly went back into the RED folder, keen to see what memory would be revealed to me. I went through the section with the older date/time stamp titles. I clicked play on the next random video and was transported to yet another vivid memory.

In primary school, I walked hand in hand with my grandma in the hallway. We were headed to my class, which was already in session. It felt like a confrontation was about to happen. My grandma had an urgent rhythm in her walk, like she was about to engage in a fist fight. I tried my best to keep up with her with my little feet as she fumed like a bull to a matador. As we opened the door to walk in, everyone was surprised to see both of us, including my teacher and at least twenty of my classmates.

My teacher looked up, startled, and shook as my grandma walked up to her table and slammed her hands on it. "My grandson told me you beat him because he lost a pencil?" Grandma said, staring right at my speechless teacher, who was evidently guilty from her outright fear of my grandmother.

The tension grew in the classroom as all the pupils looked in astonishment at how a five-foot-tall woman could bring a fearsome teacher to utter speechlessness. "When you were a student in my school, did I ever raise my hand to you? Did I ever smack you?" my grandma asked the teacher, who rapidly shook her head while mumbling incoherent whispers.

"I will report you to the headmistress for your gross negligence and bringing bodily harm to my boy. Look at his arm, for Christ's sake!" Grandma said. "Listen here, and listen good. I assure you – you will be sorry for this."

Grandma waved at me to go take a seat in the class; her protective gaze watched me all the way to my seat. As I walked by my classmates, they all smiled at me and gave little chants, like I had done something heroic. As I sat down, she gave the teacher one last intimidating stare and left the class. Within seconds, the teacher chased after her, cowering and pleading. Just as the class door shut behind the teacher, there was an uproar of amusement from the entire class, like they had just witnessed a stage play.

As the memory came to an end, I realised I had completely forgotten about this incident, but I remembered every detail as soon as I saw the video. The "Valuable lesson?" option was already set to "NO", and the text field underneath the "WHY" dialog box said, "I was scared of what the teacher would do to me afterwards for reporting her." So, I changed the valuable lesson option to "YES" and commented, "In the moment, I was worried about the aftermath. I was scared of how I would be treated in class by my teacher and the rest of my classmates. In retrospect, I now realise that it is important to stand up for those you love and to not condone abuse of any kind. I am thankful for this."

As I saved the comment, the video file glowed green and moved to the GREEN folder. Now, I'd got the hang of it.

RED meant I had nothing to be thankful for.

AMBER was for uncertainty.

GREEN meant I was thankful for the experience.

Armed with this new information, I set out to explore more of the RED and AMBER folders, to find something to be thankful for – hopefully turning as many of them GREEN as possible. As I moved from video to video, the building began to experience a mild rumble, like there was a shockwave. Then it subsided.

Undeterred, I interacted with as many videos as I possibly could. Some video memories had me crying. Some had me laughing. Some had me confused. Some had me embarrassed. With every new watch, I found a new reason to be thankful.

Thankful for learning to say "I love you" to my family.

Thankful for childhood spankings, though I reject repeating such as a parent.

Thankful for Jọlá's rebelliousness and recidivism, which challenged me to be patient.

Thankful to my brother who let me cut his hair as kids, to the disbelief of our mum.

Thankful that my grandma called me her good-luck charm.

Thankful that "Black Black Black Sheep" chants about my dark skin didn't faze me.

Thankful for family hand-me-downs, despite my love for popping tags on new outfits.

Thankful for times people forgot my birthday.

Thankful for being reluctantly obedient as a child.

Thankful to my primary school classmates for making me class captain.

Thankful for not landing on my head that one time I fell from a tree.

Thankful I wasn't hurt darting across a busy street unnoticed at age three.

Thankful that I finally stopped bed-wetting at the age of eight.

Thankful I never became a doctor, free from the burden of patient's health and fate.

Thankful for being bullied and that leading to learning self-defence and discipline.

Thankful for having a bill-paying job, despite my disdain for capitalism.

Thankful for my family, my role models, and my father figures.

Thankful for the barriers the fathers in my life broke down for me.

Thankful for every encounter that somehow led me to my wife.

Thankful for the baby on the way.

Thankful to Uncle Taj for trying to save me.

I had to stop. The neon lights above me began to flicker erratically again. The ground began to quake beneath my feet. I took my glasses and headphones off. I clutched the armrests of my seat as the room seemed to tilt and sway. Suddenly, the floor beneath me began to cave in, and I slowly sank into it as the neon lights grew brighter and brighter, almost blinding me with their intensity. A crack of thunder shook the room, paralysing me with fear as I found myself falling.

I plummeted through the ceiling of the lower floor; the impact shook the concrete and metal beneath me, sending jolts of sensation through my body as I tumbled downwards. The concrete shattered like glass, the metal twisted and buckled beneath my weight, yet I remained unscathed, my body emerging from the fall without a scratch. As I sat up from my fall, I caught a glimpse of the interviewer sitting some distance away, sipping her smoothie as if nothing were amiss. She spoke casually, as if we were still in the middle of a routine interview.

"Oh, are you done with your test now? How did you find—"

Before I could even respond, I crashed through the floor again, this time landing in the middle of a lively party. The participants were doing the *hora* dance, hoisting a young boy in a chair high above their heads. I was rooted to the spot, sitting on the ground, unable to move as the floor gave way yet again, feeling it crumble beneath me. No one took notice of me, even as I tried to apologise for crashing the party. I fell yet again through the broken concrete, in a dizzying cycle, each fall more intense than the last, the force of each impact growing stronger and stronger as I landed on the next lower floor. On this floor, I found myself in what looked like an indoor playground. Memories of my primary school came to mind as I saw children running around and playing all sorts of games. These kids were unbothered by my presence. I could hear their laughter and feel the energy of their playfulness. I had no choice but to smile as I watched them have the time of their lives.

As I sat frozen on the ground, the kids played games like Simon Says, hide and seek, musical chairs, Duck, Duck, Goose and tug of war. It was as if I had been transported back in time, to a simpler time when the biggest worry was whether or not I'd be chosen to be "it" in a game of tag.

I watched the children as they continued to play, the torrent of nostalgia washing over me. It was a bittersweet feeling, knowing that I couldn't go back to those carefree days. But for a moment, I was able to relive those memories and feel the joy of childhood once again.

Before I could stay too long in this nostalgic moment, I found myself falling again, crashing through another ceiling. The world around me shifted, whilst I prepared myself for whatever new absurdity awaited me.

As I landed on yet another floor, I saw two familiar silhouettes in the distance, two women washing dishes with their backs turned to me. I recognised them immediately as

Aunty Mimi and Grandma. They both turned their heads to acknowledge me, and I heard Grandma say, "Seesaw!", with Aunty Mimi giving a reserved smile, just before I fell through the floor once more.

I crashed yet again. But instead of landing on a hard, concrete-like surface, I was in a soft, bouncy bed. My bed. I found myself in my own bedroom, in the middle of the night, trying to make sense of the bizarre dream I'd just had. My eyes rolled to the left, and I saw my dream journal on my nightstand. I attempted to reach for it, wanting to jot down every single detail before I forgot, but something felt wrong. I couldn't move any part of my body except my eyes, which darted around the room in confusion. My eyes rolled to the right, and I saw my wife lying next to me, but I couldn't get her attention, no matter how hard I tried.

Oh God, I hope this isn't what I think it is.

It was indeed one of my greatest fears: sleep paralysis. I tried to scream, but no sound came out. It almost felt like my mouth was gagged or covered in duct tape. I imagined myself wiggling vigorously, but I had no control over any motor functions except my eyes. I looked to my side, and my wife was fast asleep. My heart began beating faster. I was desperate. I needed someone, anyone to save me.

"He—" I tried to muffle a little sound through my stiffened larynx. I barely made a sound.

"Hee—" my neck muscles and vocal cords loosened up a little, as a single tear rolled down my cheek. With my inner voice, I said a little prayer: "I know you won't let me down. I know you won't fail me." With all the energy a paralysed body could muster, I screamed, "Help me!"

I sank slowly into my bed, with my eyes closed. My body felt like it was falling yet ascending at the same time. I slowly opened my eyes to the sudden brightness of daytime, realising that I was no longer in my bed. The familiar stench of antiseptic and decay hit my nose. I heard a constant, rhythmic beeping sound and saw rays of sunlight piercing through the blinds. Similar neon lights to those in my dream subtly flashed in the corner of my eye, though not as aggressively as the lights in my dream had. My eyes struggled to adjust, and my throat felt as dry as a desert. I tried to move my legs, but they were stiff and sore. It took me a moment to realise that I was in a hospital. Of course, I had been shot.

Desperate to capture the fleeting remnants of my dream, I longed for my trusty dream journal to be within reach. Sadly, I found myself far from home, and the journal nowhere in sight. My gaze drifted to the foreign sight of a catheter attached to my arm, leading to a stand with a slow-dripping intravenous drip-bag. Pain coursed through my body, and I struggled to reach the call button to alert the nurse. The button slipped from my grasp just as I managed to press it, and I was left catching my breath and taking in the unfamiliar surroundings. Though they were subtle, and as small as pinheads, I was able to pinpoint the source of the eerie glow of coloured lights. They emanated from the life-support machine, and they flickered rhythmically, flashing in sync with the beeping sounds from the machine – it sounded like thunderclaps banging against my eardrums. I was draped in a blue hospital garment, a thin barrier between my nakedness and the world. Alarmingly, the heart monitor's waves quickened, and the beeping and flickering lights intensified, as if warning of an impending storm. I could feel my heart pounding in my chest, matching the frenzied rhythm of the monitor…

Suddenly, two nurses and a doctor rushed into the room to get me stabilised. I could breathe a sigh of a little relief. The doctor, with his stethoscope around his neck, asked me how I was feeling. I nodded, not wanting to overdo it. He checked my vital signs and asked if he could perform a pain assessment, to which I nodded again. Trying to speak, I could only manage a faint "Yes". One of the nurses jotted down notes while the other informed me that my wife was on her way up to see me.

A mix of emotions washed over me as I realised how much time had passed since the incident. The doctor asked me if I knew what day it was, and I flinched as he tapped my thighs and knees to check my sensitivity. I shook my head, whispering a "No". He then informed me that I had been in a coma for just over a month, during which time they had removed the bullet from my lower back. He checked my blood pressure and put a thermometer in my ear.

Desperately thirsty, I asked for water, and within seconds, a nurse brought me a little bottle with a straw. As I took a sip, I saw someone approaching the hospital room entrance. It was my wife, and I began to choke on the water immediately. She ran towards the bed, hugging me tightly. Shẹwà was not one to cry easily, but her emotions got the better of her. Finally, a familiar face.

"Oh, babe, you had me so worried," she said, her voice breaking. "I'm so happy to see you awake," she continued.

"I've been here every day since—" Shẹwà was interrupted by something the doctor must have said. "How is he, doctor?" she asked.

"So far, so good. We will have to do some imaging tests and neurological exams to get a full prognosis," he replied.

As Shẹwà turned away to listen to the medical jargon, I was drawn to her beauty, her scent, and her glow. She had bags under her eyes – they were puffy from crying or lack of sleep. I kept glancing at her as it hit me – the memories of the incident flooded my mind. I remembered my bloody hands holding her pregnancy bump. "Oh no," I said, and Shẹ̀wà swiftly turned her head towards me. I reached my catheter arm over her belly, placing my hand on it.

"Where's the baby?"

Chapter 16

Shẹ̀wà

"AK, are you okay? Babe!" I said in the most concerned tone I had probably ever used with him.

"Don't worry about it, my love. Let's just get to the car," Akándé said, still trying to protect me when he was clearly the one who needed safeguarding.

"Hmph, the baby," I said under my breath, feeling the baby kick restlessly. Akándé instinctively placed his hands on my belly. He was bleeding a lot – his blood was all over my lavender-coloured dress. As I wrapped my arm around his back, I could feel the damp warm pool of blood as he began to slip to the floor.

"Akándé! Akándé!" Mama B began to repetitively scream his name. He staggered, collapsing to the ground. I felt helpless; I was too big to be agile.

As he lay there, I kneeled next to him. I ignored all the gunfire and was prepared to stay with him, no matter what. Everything seemed to move in slow motion after that. There was so much screaming, I could barely hear myself calling for Jọlá. They were a few metres in front; Uncle Taj turned around, hesitated at first, then left Jọlá and Dámi while motioning for them to keep going. Akándé's uncle lifted him up and carried him into his Toyota. I sat in the back seat of the unfamiliar

179

vehicle, holding Akándé's hand. Mama B kept muttering what sounded like prayers under her breath as she carefully placed Akándé's head on my lap; she then proceeded to sit in the front passenger's seat, while Uncle Taj adjusted Akándé's lower body to fit the car perfectly. We couldn't all fit in Uncle Taj's Toyota. As he entered the driver's seat and shut the door, Dámi and Jọlá both began shouting, "Shẹ̀wà, keys, give us the keys to the Honda."

"I don't have them," I said.

"AK's pockets. Check his pockets!" The howling sound of police car sirens became audible in the distance as I searched Akándé's pockets for the car keys.

"Please hurry up, we need to leave now!" Uncle Taj shouted.

"Dámi, are you sure you can drive the car?" I asked with genuine concern.

"Yes. It's an automatic drive, right? Don't worry, we're gonna drive right behind you," Dámi reassured. I found the car keys just in time and tossed them to Dámi. Jọlá had tears streaming down her face, looking around frantically, probably to ensure they were not in harm's way. Dámi grabbed Jọlá's hand, and they got into the Honda faster than I could turn my neck around to track them. Uncle Taj drove off. He swerved the car back and forth – it was a surprise Dámi could keep up.

I could feel Akándé's pulse weakening. We arrived at the hospital, and Akándé was rushed to the emergency room, taken from us by the staff. I stayed with him, refusing to leave his side. My mind began racing with thoughts of my husband's life hanging in the balance. The doctors wheeled Akándé to the operating theatre. The bullet had lodged close to his spine, and they had to induce a coma to remove it. I kept getting phone calls but ignored them. Mama B, Jǫlá, and Dámi urged me to go home and rest.

I told them, "I'm not leaving."

"You have to think of the baby, you know," Dámi said.

"Baby will be fine. Better to be here than at home. I would be restless. And if anything happens, to me or the baby, well, good thing we're already in a hospital."

Jǫlá, Dámi, and Mama B conceded.

I couldn't bear the thought of being away from him, not knowing what might happen. His operation was over in four hours. I was told there were complications in the surgery, that due to those complications, Akándé would need to wake up from the coma himself, so as not to send him into unnecessary shock. I stayed next to him in recovery. I nodded off several times, and the nurses tried to make me feel comfortable, seeing as I was too stubborn to want to leave. They gave me pillows, a footrest, and even access to the TV in Akándé's room. He was intubated, hooked up to a drip and a life-support system. I would stare at him, speak to him, hold his hand. I needed him to know I was by his side. As I switched on the TV, the room filled with the glow of the screen, casting an unsettling translucence on my bloodstained clothes. I could feel the weight of my husband's hand in mine as I sat by his hospital bed, his comatose body a stark reminder of the violence that had erupted at the cemetery earlier that day.

The news report flashed images of the chaos that had ensued, the screams of the wounded and the wails of the mourning echoing in my ears. A knot formed in my stomach as I saw the number of casualties – five dead, eleven injured, my husband among them.

As the reporter relayed the details of the attack, I felt grateful for my own survival. A mix of relief and guilt consumed me. The assailants had been caught according to the news, but their motives remained unknown. *Was it a senseless act of violence? A petty squabble or gang-related retaliation?* I tried not to dwell on it, focusing instead on the hope that my husband would wake up soon.

Despite him being shot in the back, I was optimistic about his recovery, refusing to let fear consume me. As I held his hand, I felt his warmth, a reminder of the life that still coursed through him. I knew that it wouldn't be easy, but I was determined to see him through this, to keep him safe, and to cherish every moment we had together.

In that moment, surrounded by the beeps and hums of the hospital machines, I was reminded of the fragility of life and the importance of holding on to hope. As I closed my eyes, I sent up a silent prayer, asking for strength and for a future filled with love and joy, despite the uncertainty.

Coincidentally, the same hospital I was in was where I had planned to have our baby. I even had a scan due the next day. It was only about a five-minute walk from the intensive care unit to the maternity ward. I was getting a little restless sitting down.

I could do with the exercise.

As I attempted to stand up, I was forced to sit back down due to the sharp pain in my belly. It wasn't the baby kicking. It was probably just Braxton-Hicks contractions. I attempted to stand up again, and this time there was no pain. *Hallelujah.*

"We'll be back soon," I said to Akándé while cradling my bump, as I tried to imagine what he would say back to me. I hoped to find a vending machine with snacks. I took only five steps out of Akándé's room, and the pain I'd felt previously was dialled up to a hundred this time. I screamed. The nurses came to get me. They put me in a wheelchair, and as soon as I told them I was registered for maternity care at the hospital, they took me to the maternity ward.

The results of my scans suggested I had very high blood pressure and would need an emergency caesarean section, due to the high risks of preeclampsia and accumulated stress. Despite my protests of not being ready, I was rushed into the delivery room, where I gave birth to a premature baby boy. He looked so much like his daddy. I couldn't hold him for too long. He was so small, only weighed about two kilograms. The joy of having a child was overshadowed by the fear that my son might not survive. He was placed in intensive care, sectioned off into an incubator room with others like him. I alternated visits between my husband and my newborn.

One month after the shooting, Akándé still hadn't woken up, and the baby was still in the hospital. I was breast pumping one day to provide milk for the baby, when a nurse called me to come to AK's ward. He was awake!

I couldn't contain my joy. I dropped everything I was doing. I hadn't planned for this moment; I was just taking it one day at a time. *But what if he doesn't remember me?* I thought.

I ran as fast as my legs could take me, burst into the room. I could immediately tell from his eyes that he recognised me. I hugged Akándé tightly, tears streaming down my face.

Compose yourself, I thought, trying not to cry in front of strangers.

"Oh, babe, you had me so worried. I'm so happy to see you awake."

"How is he, doctor?" I asked.

"So far, so good. We will have to do some imaging tests and neurological exams to get a full prognosis, to understand a potential road to recovery," the doctor replied. Akándé had that same stare, like there was something on his mind, but he was struggling to find the right words for it.

"Where's the baby?" he asked.

"The baby is fine." I told him how I'd had an emergency c-section, along with practically living in the hospital for a month. During that time, I watched over the baby like a hawk, unable to hold him due to his placement in the incubator. Akándé was desperate to see him, leaning forward, trying to move his legs off the bed, but he struggled so much, with one leg more than the other. He couldn't stand up if he wanted to.

"Relax, AK, you'll see him in due time," I said, as I tried to ease him back into bed. "Right now, you need your strength back."

"Your wife is right. No need to be an eager beaver," the doctor said. "Please try to rest. We will prep you for an MRI scan and then get you some food to eat."

Akándé complied. The doctor and nurses left the room, and they would be back in a few minutes to continue with other tests.

As I sat next to him, holding his hand, I realised for the first time how much his beard had grown. He had become so lean that I wondered if he would have any appetite.

"What would you like to eat?" I asked.

"I wanna make a phone call," he said abruptly, completely ignoring what I had just said.

"Huh?"

"Can I make a call, please?"

He requested a video call with his uncle, the man who had saved his life. It had just occurred to me that I hadn't told anyone else he was awake. Most people knew he was in a coma – his work, church, our entire family and friends. I had kept his phone with me, answering most incoming calls on his behalf, until I got tired of people asking me questions like *Is he awake yet?* Or *What are the doctors saying?*

I helped sit him up to make the call. His face was drawn and weary. He adjusted his position, trying to find some comfort as he held his phone to his ear at first. But then his uncle's face appeared on the video call instead. I took the phone and held it in place for him, making sure he was in frame, while I stayed at an angle next to him.

"Hello, Uncle," Akándé said, his voice hoarse.

"Akándé! You're finally awake!" The uncle's face lit up, and he leaned closer to the camera. "How are you feeling, my boy?"

"I'm… I'm doing okay," Akándé said, though he still looked weak. "Thanks… Thank you for helping me get to the hospital. I wouldn't be here without you."

The uncle nodded solemnly. "That's what family does; the ties that bind us are unbreakable."

Akándé's expression softened with gratitude. "I owe you so much, Uncle… I don't know how to repay you."

"You don't need to repay me, Akándé," his uncle said gently. "You're family. I was just doing what any family member would do."

Akándé looked down at his hands, twisting the bedsheet between his fingers. "I need to talk to you about something, Uncle. I've been carrying a lot of guilt about what happened with Jọlá and the whole child-custody-battle thing."

His uncle's face became serious, and he leaned forward. "Akándé, you don't need to apologise. I've made peace with that matter a long time ago. So please, let go of your guilt. I don't hold any grudges against you."

Akándé's eyes widened in surprise, and he looked up at his uncle. "I was actually going to call a truce rather than apologise." There was static interference in the video call, a glitch that may have paused the video for a quick second.

"What was that?" his uncle asked firmly.

"Never mind, please continue what you were saying." Akándé deflected the question.

"I was saying, you did what you had to do, and I can't blame you for fighting to keep your word to your aunt. It's totally understandable."

Akándé let out a deep breath, as if a heavy weight had been lifted off his chest. Though I couldn't tell if he was being completely genuine or just being courteous. "Thank you, Uncle. I feel undeserving. But less guilty. Thank you."

Uncle Taj smiled gently. "I'm glad, Akándé. You don't need to carry that burden anymore. You just focus on getting better, okay? You have a little boy to take care of."

Akándé nodded, tears forming in his eyes. "Yeah, you're right. I have a lot to be grateful for."

The uncle let out a hearty chuckle, a pleased expression crossing his face. "Ẹ̀hẹ́n! That's the spirit, Akándé. You'll get through this, and we'll all be here to support you."

Akándé acknowledged with a smile, and I could see the gratitude on his face. "Thanks, Uncle. I'm glad I can call you family."

The call ended.

Soon enough, the nurses came to take Akándé away for the MRI scan, so I went off to go attend to the baby. I hadn't named him yet, though I had secretly been referring to him as Akándé Junior, or AJ, despite my distaste for the "Junior" moniker. It didn't feel right naming him without Akándé's input, yet I had to refer to the baby somehow. Saying "the baby" all the time got tiresome quickly. On my way to see AJ, I called Mama B,

Dámi, and Jǫlá to tell them the news. They were overjoyed and planned to come the next morning.

The next morning, the doctors requested my audience to discuss Akándé's test results, therefore I left home alone earlier than expected. Mama B, Dámi, and Jǫlá were still getting ready, so I had to leave them. They could find their way. I had gone home the night before to get a proper shower. Since my postnatal discharge, I hadn't been allowed to sleep at the hospital. My pregnant-lady privileges were gone. That meant I had to commute from home to the hospital and back daily. I didn't mind, as long as I got to spend time with my two-favourite people. AJ was looking good, and there was talk of removing him from his incubator. *I could hold him soon.* The thought alone made me euphoric.

I was also hopeful about Akándé's recovery. He had complained about intermittent stiffness on the left side of his body. He would lose balance when he tried to stand up, and couldn't walk without some sort of support. When I arrived at the hospital, I went to Akándé's ward first. He wore a smile. The breakfast he'd had a few hours ago must've given him a boost of energy.

"Hey, my love," Akándé said, sounding more like himself today. I realised how much I'd missed his voice.

"Hey, babe. How are you?" I asked with genuine concern. Seeing as the room was already filled with a few doctors, we kept our chat brief. He only responded to me with a nod. He was as eager as I was to hear the doctors' overall medical report and analysis. One of them handed me a letter about Akándé's diagnosis, because I had been asking for a medical letter on behalf of his workplace, so he could apply for sick leave. It would have been a shame if they put a hold on his salary due to missing work for over a month.

Dear Mr Akándé Jímọ̀h

Medical Report

Diagnosis: Brown-Séquard syndrome

Cause: Penetrating trauma by bullet injury.

Observations: Partial lesions in spine. Partially severed pyramidal and spinothalamic tracts.

– Ipsilateral loss of proprioception and vibration sensations.

– Ipsilateral upper motor neuron deficit (weakness) secondary to interruption of the corticospinal tract.

– Contralateral loss of crude touch, pain, and temperature due to spinothalamic tracts.

Prognosis: With a planned rehabilitation, ambulation could take 3 to 6 months.

The doctor's words hit me like a boulder. "We ran a comprehensive set of tests," he said, "and I'm sorry to inform you that the results indicate that you have Brown-Séquard syndrome. It's because of the injury you sustained when you were shot in the back. The condition affects the way your spinal cord works, causing weakness, numbness, or paralysis on one side of your body – in your case, your left side. You may also experience pain and discomfort in that area."

Feeling overwhelmed, I turned to hold Akándé's hand firmly, hoping to reassure him that I was there for him, no matter what. But the doctor continued, promising to help us manage the condition with a personalised treatment plan that included physical therapy, medication, and other supportive measures.

I felt a knot in my throat, but I refused to let despair take over. Shortly after receiving the news, I requested a wheelchair from one of the regular nurses who knew me. I told Akándé I wanted him to get some fresh air, and he agreed. But getting him onto the chair was harder than I expected. The nurse made it look easy, and she was being a little too nice to my husband.

"I think she likes you, AK," I teased, trying to distract Akándé from his probable lingering thoughts of his diagnosis. But I had something up my sleeve, and soon we were on our way to the paediatric ward, where our son was. Eagerly waiting were Mama B, Jọlá, and Dámi. They had flowers and balloons – one balloon had the words "Welcome back to the land of the living" on it, a touch of Dámi's sense of humour.

As everyone showered Akándé with hugs and kisses, Jọlá joked that he was overdue for a haircut and a shave. Akándé laughed and asked if she could bring his hair clipper, his dream journal, and a blank unused notepad next time she visited. But my surprise wasn't over yet. I wheeled Akándé towards the incubation room, where our son lay. As Akándé placed his hands firmly on the glass window barrier, his emotions overwhelmed him. "Oh, my boy," he said with so much longing.

Within the next week, our baby was discharged from the hospital, and we decided on a name for him: Dúròtìmí, alternatively Ròtìmí for short, which meant "stand by me".

Akándé was discharged with a wheelchair and a pair of crutches. His left leg hurt too much to stand on, but if he stuck to his rehabilitation over the next few months, he would be able to do things more independently.

— ∞ —

Back at home, I struggled to cope with the baby, Akándé's condition, and my own state of mind. Mama B, Jọlá, and Dámi helped out, but they had their own lives to live. Mama B had to return to Nigeria because her UK visa would soon expire. Jọlá had school exams coming up, so she was of little help at home. Dámi, aware of our financial constraints, had shown some interest in Akándé's African-textile-inspired watches and said she would take the reins of the marketing and logistics, to reinvigorate the business with Akándé's blessing. This meant she had to make a few trips, in addition to going back to Lagos to complete her final year in university. We were thankful to her, but with that, I had no help. I sometimes felt alone and isolated in my own thoughts, silently fighting depression and postnatal stress. I was taking care of everything and everyone, from helping Akándé with going to the toilet to changing nappies for both my husband and baby. It was a lot to handle, and I wouldn't wish it on my worst enemy.

As I cradled Ròtìmí in my embrace, a groundswell of overwhelming emotions came over me. Akándé, who had been my rock and support, was now the one who needed my help. With his unpredictable left side, it meant I had to assist him with everything.

One morning, as I was changing Ròtìmí's nappy, I heard a loud thump while I was in the bedroom. It came from the bathroom. It sounded like Akándé had fallen and needed my help. I rushed to his side and tried to lift him, but his weight was too much for me. A sharp pain pierced through my back, forcing me to rest for a while before attempting again. I knew that I had to be careful with my movements from then on, as my own physical health was important too.

Caring for my husband also meant providing emotional support. It was hard to see him frustrated and depressed about his condition. I tried to be there for him, to listen and offer words of encouragement, but sometimes it felt like I wasn't doing enough. It was a constant battle to keep him motivated and hopeful.

Managing my husband's medical care was another challenge. We had to schedule regular doctor's visits, manage his medications, and arrange for physical therapy. It was frustrating for Akándé at first, but he became encouraged once he saw some of the progress he was making. I had to juggle this with my baby's needs, often taking Ròtìmí with us to the appointments. It was tiring, but I knew it was necessary for my husband's recovery.

The financial strain was also a heavy burden. Akándé had been unable to work for three months now, and the cost of medical care and assistive devices was adding up. I had to manage our finances and seek financial assistance wherever possible. Thankfully, his workplace agreed to have him work from home, and they sent over some helpful gear to get him started, like an adjustable desk and chair, an ergonomic keyboard, a mouse, and a laptop with in-built speech recognition software.

The stigma and social isolation that came with my husband's condition affected me too. People didn't always know how to behave in our presence. At times, it seemed as though I was being judged for being a caregiver. Not how I had hoped to spend my maternity leave. It was a lonely feeling, but I knew that I had to stay strong for my husband and our family.

All of these challenges took a toll on me, and I found myself wallowing in depression. All the signs were there. It probably wasn't healthy to self-diagnose, but I knew I had to seek help and support for myself, even as I continued to care for my husband and baby.

— ∞ —

It was 3 am one night. My insomnia had come back to haunt me. Ròtìmí had just begun to teethe, and he wouldn't stop crying. Akándé was fast asleep; he didn't move a muscle. I put Ròtìmí's dummy in his mouth and placed him back in his cot. I decided I needed to clear my head. I needed a walk. In one of my most out-of-character moments, I opened the front door, stepped out, and just started walking. A certain darkness engulfed me as I walked away from my house. The cool night air seemed to wrap around me like a comforting blanket, yet I was numb to its touch. My mind was racing with a million thoughts, each one pushing me closer and closer to the edge.

I left behind my crying five-month-old baby and my paralysed husband, who was sound asleep, oblivious to my departure. For the first time in a long time, I was free and unfazed.

As I walked, I passed by familiar streets that I had walked countless times before. But tonight, everything seemed different. The streetlights flickered above me, casting ghostly shadows across the pavement. The only sounds were the rustling of leaves and the distant hum of cars.

As I walked, the confusion in my mind began to clear. The darkness that had been consuming me started to lift, and I had a moment of clarity. I realised that I couldn't keep running away from my problems. That I couldn't keep ignoring the help that was available to me.

I stopped in my tracks, took a deep breath, and turned around. I knew I had to go back. I had to face my fears and confront the challenges that lay ahead. As I walked back towards my house, I felt at ease. The streetlights no longer seemed threatening, but instead, they provided a guiding light. The rustling leaves now sounded comforting, like they were whispering words of encouragement. And the hum of cars in the distance now sounded like a gentle murmur, reminding me that I wasn't alone.

When I reached our driveway, I saw my husband holding our baby at the front door. He looked up and saw me, relief flooding his face.

"What happened? Where did you go?" Akándé said in a demanding yet monotone voice. "At this time? With Ròtìmí crying?" Each question hit me like a dagger. "You know, I actually thought you were gone. Like, gone for good."

"Why would you think that?" I questioned him, cunningly ignoring his previous questions.

"You know, I've heard stories of mothers who just up and leave, and never turn back," he said as he patted Ròtìmí and lowered his voice so as not to wake the baby up.

"I would never do that." I didn't believe my own words. He probably didn't either.

"Look, I know these past few months have been a struggle. You have been my pillar, my rock and—"

"Sometimes I feel like he doesn't even like me," I interrupted Akándé, while looking down at Ròtìmí, surprised by how he was still asleep despite our not-so-quiet conversation. Akándé was still staring at me like he was finding it hard to comprehend what I had just said. I finally shut the front door and locked up, and I motioned for Akándé to head into the living room to continue our talk.

"How so?" he finally said after sitting in a comfortable position and palming Ròtìmí's head close.

"Well, you seem to have the magic touch. He never cries when you carry him. He cries all the time with me, and he's rejected my milk so many times. To the point where I'm no longer able to produce. Hence why we've had to move to formula. I know you help out a lot as well, despite your condition, but I just never feel like it's enough." Akándé's finger brushed my cheek, wiping away a tear. I'd thought I was doing so well holding back my emotions. The thoughts that kept going through my mind were *I've failed as a mother. I've failed as a wife.* I wondered if he'd ever be able to forgive me.

"You know, a baby communicating to a parent is like playing charades with someone who doesn't understand the rules of the game." He analogised his way into making me smile when he said that.

"Reminds me of someone I know who's bad at charades," I responded, trying to keep the joke and the analogy alive. He chuckled at a volume low enough to keep the baby sleeping.

"We're definitely teaching him to play when he gets older," he said as he used his shaky left hand to hold my arm. "Listen, remember you can always talk to me. Never let things get to a breaking point, I beg of you," he pleaded. I acknowledged by nodding. "You are not a bad mother, and Ròtìmí does not dislike you; he is still figuring out his own emotions. We are the sum of our individual and collective experiences. Everything you've learned up till the point of his birth prepared you to be a good mother. Everything you are learning now is making you into a better mother. You might judge and critique yourself, but remember, what you learn today makes you better tomorrow." He paused. But he wasn't done.

"So, when we have another baby, for instance, knowing full well every baby is unique, you will carry over some life lessons from caring for Ròtìmí into taking care of that new child. Motherhood and fatherhood are a continuum reinforced by the passage of time." He stopped, trying to measure my facial expressions, to see if he was getting through to me with his profound message.

"Sounds like you're trying to get in my pants with all this talk of another baby," I joked dismissively. Akándé laughed so uncontrollably that he woke Ròtìmí up this time. I reached over to take him from Akándé.

"Well, is it working?" he queried enticingly.

"Maybe." I smirked.

"But seriously, though, was I able to get through to you?" His face turned serious as I tried to pat the baby back to sleep.

"Yeah, don't worry, I got all you said. Mother-father-time-continuum. Father Time. Mother Nature. Solid speech," I joked dismissively again as Ròtìmí continued to cry, and I got up to go make a bottle of formula for him. I realised how much I had almost lost in one night. I'd honestly thought Akándé would be angrier at me, but he'd made me feel safe with his words. For the first time in months, I felt seen. I knew that this was just the beginning of a long journey, and thankfully, I knew I wasn't alone.

As I took one last look at him before leaving the living room with Ròtìmí, I saw him shaking his head at me, smiling, and then saying, "You're such a joker."

Chapter 17

Akándé's Tape #22: unedited transcript

Akándé: (coughs) Sitting in my dimly lit home office, staring at the stack of audio recordings on my desk, I can't help but feel anxious. Some of these recordings contain interviews with each of my parents and their own life experiences, but more importantly, accounts of how they met and how their affair led to my birth. At different instances during my convalescence, they came to my home to check on me. They agreed to sit with me, to discuss the past, while I recorded. The emotions in their voices are palpable. Well, more palpable emotions when it comes to my mum. Dad was a little reluctant to participate in these conversations with me. "It's for posterity" were the words I used to finally convince him… I hold the several-hours-long audio tapes in my hand as I keep staring at the labels on the front: "Mum Interview #1" and "Dad Interview #1". My heart races as I attempt to press the play button on the cassette player, knowing the fresh memories of the recording sessions will come back to me.

(long pause)

Akándé: (continues) Most of what I know about my childhood or events that transpired before my time was only able to remain in my recollection due to an amalgamation of frequent trips down memory lane with different family members, family photo albums, memorabilia, and formative experiences. (sniffs) Listening back to these recordings is akin to an emotional rollercoaster for me. On one hand, it's fascinating to hear my parents' stories in their own words, to gain insight into their lives before I was born. On the other hand, it's difficult to hear about the struggles they faced, the pain they endured, and the mistakes they made. Hearing their voices again feels like reliving the original live recording sessions.

(long pause)

Akándé: (exhales) But despite the emotional toll, listening to these recordings has also reminded me of a decision I made as a child. A decision to be a great husband and father, to learn from the imperfections of my parents and create a different kind of path for myself. Hearing my parents' stories has only strengthened my resolve to be the kind of man I always wanted to be... And so, as I sit here contemplating whether to transcribe these recordings into the first chapter of my book, I know that it won't be easy. But I also know that it's a story that needs to be told, a story that will resonate with so many others who have faced similar struggles and made similar decisions. (inhales) Hence, with a deep breath and an outpouring of purpose, I begin the daunting task of turning these recordings into something more.

(gadgetry click)

— ∞ —

Dad Interview #1. Start time 00:04:34

Dad: I'd like to start with a story... (sighs) So once upon a time, as the story goes, a lively young boy adored his parents and lived with his three other siblings. Despite being the youngest, he was the family's source of comic relief. He had an intense desire for adventure and often begged his dad to take him along on errands, and his dad eventually obliged. On one such occasion, the father made an unplanned stop, leaving the boy waiting in the car for what seemed like an eternity. Upon his return, the boy witnessed his dad with an unknown lady, engaging in flirtations that he knew crossed the boundaries of marriage. His father warned him sternly not to tell his mother, but the boy could not keep such a secret… Are you with me so far?

Akándé: (mumbles) Mm-hmm, yes.

Dad: When the wife confronted this same father, he denied the allegations. Within months, the unknown lady got pregnant. The marriage experienced a strain, but it remained resilient. Nevertheless, the father resented his son's betrayal and projected his insecurities and guilt onto him, scolding and smacking him for things he didn't do, well into his teenage years. This maltreatment made the son question his father's love and even contemplate the worst. The father's condemnation of the son's betrayal pushed the son towards making intricate plans to end his own life, but those plans were thwarted by his keen-eyed mother. (coughs repeatedly)

Akándé: Do you want some water?

Dad: No thank you.

Akándé: Okay, let me know if you do. Please continue.

Dad: (grunts) Years went by, and this son got to know his half-brother, who was the spitting image of himself, and they would eventually become close. The son never felt remorse from his father, who remained oblivious to his oppressive acts of intimidation towards his son. Thirty years later, with children of his own, the son one day confronted his father about his past transgressions. The father played clueless, easily chalking it up to the son's failed memory or belittling his son's perspective of events… Despite my denial, I know the pain and scars of my actions still linger with him. Yet, he probably shows me the most kindness out of all my children. (exhales)

Akándé: Do you regret not admitting to my brother that you were wrong or could've handled things better?

Dad: There's nothing to admit. I can't change what happened in the past, but I do admit that things could've been handled better.

Akándé: But surely you recognise the extent to which he was affected by all of this. Don't you want to resolve any resentment and be at peace with him, given that you are fully aware of the whole ordeal he has been through, including the mental and psychological torture?

Dad: Sure, I admit to being obstinate once in a while.

Akándé: Once in a while?

Dad: (grunts) Yes, once in a while. Nevertheless, bringing up the past is a waste of time if it won't change anything. I regret nothing. I loved your mother and wanted to tell my wife about the affair on my own terms. Your brother robbed me of that. So, whatever I did to him wasn't premeditated, but a lesson in loyalty.

Akándé: But did you consider the impact you would have on his impressionable mind and how it would affect the man he would become?

Dad: Perhaps.

Akándé: Was that Kùnlé in your story?

Dad: (coughs) Obviously.

Akándé: I believe you should talk to him about this. Let him know why you did what you did. Dad, we have come a long way from fathers acting tough around their sons because they are afraid to appear weak. It is clear, through your story, that this has weighed heavily on your mind. The least you could do, even if you don't admit to any wrongdoing, is to agree with him that things could have gone better. Don't you think so?

Dad: Maybe.

Akándé: Sorry for stating the obvious, but you're not getting any younger. Please don't be like those elderly people who begin to yearn, confess, and wallow in lifelong regrets on their deathbeds.

Dad: Don't be ridiculous. I might be an octogenarian, but I'll still race you and win.

Akándé: Haha, I'd like to see you try.

Dad: (laughs)

Akándé: (continues laughing, then pauses) Did you ever wish you could have spent more time with me when I was growing up?

Dad: (exhales) Son, all the time. I always wished I could have spent more time with you, but your mother's parents were very protective of you, and I didn't want to cause any more trouble.

Akándé: (voice cracking) I missed you a lot. But I'm grateful for all the time we eventually did spend together.

Dad: I'm grateful for those times too, son. And now that you have a son of your own, I know you understand just how important it is to be a good father.

Akándé: (exhales)

Dad: Listen… There's something I need to tell you. Something I've been keeping from you all these years… I didn't just try to see you more often, as a baby, I forcefully tried to take you away from your grandparents and your mother. I wanted you to be with me all the time. I believed it was better for you to live in a nuclear family unit... you know... one where there were married parents and siblings in one home. My plans were foiled, hence why my visits to you as a child were very limited.

Akándé: Basically, you tried to kidnap me?

Dad: (mumbles) Sounds harsh when you say it like that.

Akándé: Not harsh at all, just calling a spade a spade by trying to make logical sense of this. Because I remember the daredevil stunt you pulled in my secondary school, when you took me without Grandma's permission as she stood nearby.

Dad: You came willingly, that's hardly kidnapping...

Akándé: (shrieks) You tricked me. I loved you, and you tricked me. I ached to be with you always, but you should've thought of better ways of going about things than tricking people. Imagine being a victim of Stockholm syndrome to my own father!

Dad: I'm sorry, Akándé... I know I should have told you this a long time ago. But I didn't want to hurt you. Plus, I'm guessing your mother and grandparents probably never told you because they wanted to protect your image of me. I just wanted to be a part of your life. And I realise that you can't force a relationship; it needs to be mutual.

Akándé: Dad... It's all good. What you've said means a lot, and I'm just glad you're here now.

Dad Interview #1. Pause time 00:22:35

— ∞ —

Akándé: (sniffs) There are a lot more hours of audio recordings from my father, but I believe that is a good point to pause and possibly return later. The interview made me question a lot of the things I thought I knew as a child. Perchance my memories and what I thought I remembered have been repressed, reinterpreted positively, maybe even dissociated due to certain traumas. That is why getting multiple opinions to confirm past events is usually recommended when recalling one's childhood. These are the thoughts that linger in my mind as I hit the pause button… (sighs) The process of transcribing can be both meditative and frustrating. Meditative in that there's a certain rhythm to the act of writing out the words I hear, almost like a musical score being written in real time. Frustrating in that there are moments when the voices blur together or the words become indistinct, and I have to strain to make out what's being said, or hit the rewind/replay button to get it right. Sometimes, I even end up filling the gaps and making assumptions for any unheard words. The process feels arduous, but I will persevere.

(long pause)

Akándé: I'm going to take a quick break, stretch and grab a glass of water, to get ready for the next tape.

(receding footsteps)

— ∞ —

Mum Interview #1. Start time 00:34:39

Mum: (exhales) Okay, so I had just come out of a long-term relationship and was frustrated with being single in my twenties, while most of my friends had already started their own families. I wanted something more meaningful than just a flimsy fling, but I had my guard up around most people outside of my family. The constant questions from family about my love life only added to my anxiety. (sniffs) One day, my father, who as you know was a lawyer, asked me to drop off some case files at a fellow lawyer's chambers. I went there with my cousin. The whole time I was there, I sensed the constant gaze of the lawyer-man, your father, on me, which made me feel uncomfortable. As we were about to leave the office, he stopped me and asked for a quick word. I told my cousin to go ahead, that I would catch up with her later. The lawyer…

Akándé: Hang on… I always thought in this story, you went to the office alone?

Mum: Oh no, I didn't. I went along with my cousin Wùrà. She came to my dad's office to visit me that day and tagged along with me everywhere I went the entire day.

Akándé: Apologies for interrupting, please continue.

Mum: So where did I stop? (sniffs) Oh yes, I told my cousin to go ahead, that I would catch up with her later. He said he would like to get to know me better. Despite my reservations, I reluctantly agreed to meet up with him at a later date. I knew he was married and had four kids, and that my parents would never approve of our relationship. But something about him was alluring and inexplicable. Our friendship eventually turned into an affair, but we were careful to keep it a secret. Our clandestine relationship didn't stay a secret for long. I became pregnant and was faced with the difficult decision of keeping the baby or not. I was very indecisive, but told no one… I made two trips to different abortion clinics while in my fourth month of pregnancy, and I was turned away both times due to the risks of a late termination. So, in the end, (sniffs) I decided to keep the baby. I mustered up the courage to tell my mother, who was furious but supportive. My father, on the other hand, disowned me and kicked me out of his house.

Akándé: (mumbles)

Mum: What was that?

Akándé: I said, 'classic Grandpa', but don't mind me, please continue.

Mum: Okay. So, I had to move in with my older sister, who had four children of her own, including a newborn girl. Astonishingly, your father asked for my hand in marriage, and thought he was being honourable by doing so. I thought he was funny and never took his proposal seriously. He even had the audacity to present his proposal to my parents, who, for obvious reasons, were outraged at the idea of polygamy and banished him from ever visiting their house… I focused on my pregnancy and just wanted peace of mind until my baby arrived. Finally, you were born, weighing 3.4 kilos, on a Friday at 1:15 am at a hospital close to my sister's home, same place she gave birth to all her kids. (sniffs) We celebrated with a naming ceremony, but your father, knowing he was still banned from visitations, sent over his desired names for you. My mother, your grandma, tore up the piece of paper he sent over with his desired names and insisted that I would be the one to name you. Therefore, I named you 'Akándé', which means 'my firstborn' and also means 'a child birthed on purpose, with purpose'. You were not a mistake.

Akándé: (gasps)

Mum: Not long after you were born, my father, your grandfather, welcomed me back home and said he would support me, as long as I promised to further my education into law. I promised. But I lied. Your grandpa was so desperate for one of his children to be a lawyer, and I was desperate for a home for my child. Despite the difficult circumstances, I knew that you deserved all the love and attention I could give.

Akándé: Wow, I was today years old when I realised my name was associated with purpose… Makes me love my name even more now… I've also heard that the name 'Akándé' could also mean 'he who comes after the first sexual encounter between a father and a mother'. Is there any association between this meaning and my conception too?

Mum: (muttering) Well… I, err… I think that was pure coincidence, but come to think of it, it is quite possible that meaning holds credence too.

Akándé: Mum… why have you never told me about contemplating abortion before?

Mum: (exhales) I suppose I never found the right time to bring it up. But I'm glad you asked that we revisit the past.

Akándé: I love you, Mum.

Mum: (giggles) I love you too, Akándé mí.

Akándé: You know, for the longest time, I longed to hear you say 'I love you'… I mean, we say it to each other now as adults, but you never really said it to me as a child. Even though your actions and expressions always made me feel loved, hearing it from you as an adult means the world to me. I'm glad this is being recorded… haha!

Mum: It's true, I suppose I'm not the most outspoken when it comes to expressing my emotions. (whimpers) But you played a huge part in helping me become more comfortable with saying those words out loud. And for that, I'm grateful.

Akándé: (whispers) Thank you for choosing me as your child. I couldn't imagine anyone else being my mother.

Mum: From the moment I held you in my arms, I knew you were special… You were such a good baby, hardly ever fussy.

And as you grew up, you became such an assertive yet humble young man. You have always been a blessing, never a burden. And I thank God for you every day.

Akándé: That means so much to me, Mum.

(long pause)

Akándé: Wow, who knew you had a way with words?

Mum: (giggles) I was an English teacher, remember? It's in my blood.

Akándé: I'm glad you said that, because I have something I want to read to you. I want you to tell me what you think… It's a poem. (coughs and inhales)

I owe my life to the chance of being born
For without it, I would never have known
The flaws that make me who I am today
Nor the fears I've faced along the way.
Confronting them was not an easy task
But it gave me direction when I didn't know my path
And through my journey, I've seen the world
And questioned what my potential holds.
Dreams keep me going, and persistence is key
But patience is what allows me to truly see
The truth that lies within me
And the persona that I must unveil.
With belief in myself, I've found my strengths
And discovered the gifts that life brings
Appreciating them each and every day
And counting the blessings that come my way.

Akándé: (exhales) What's wrong?

Mum: (sniffling and muttering) Nothing… It's… It's just that I was just thinking about how scared I was when you were in that coma. I thought I was going to lose you forever.

Akándé: I'm sorry, Mum. I didn't mean to upset you.

Mum: No, no, it's not your fault... From the day you were born, you gave me so much meaning. And even though this wasn't the first time I was scared of losing you, the shooting, the coma, the paralysis – the fear of losing you this time was the most terrifying feeling I've ever felt. Your life hanging in the balance even made Taj and me make amends. I've buried too many of my own people, and I don't think I could cope with burying my own child.

Akándé: I'm here, Mum... I'm okay.

Mum: I know... But you better try your very best to stay out of harm's way.

Akándé: I will, Mum... I promise.

(faint sound of a baby crying in the background)

Akándé: Wait, do you hear that?

Mum: (pauses) Yes, I do. Is it coming from upstairs?

(crying grows louder and closer)

Akándé: That sounds like Ròtìmí crying. Is Shẹ̀wà with him?

Mum: I'm not sure. Let me go check.

(knocking)

Shẹ̀wà: So sorry to interrupt. But can I get some help with Ròtìmí? I really need to use the bathroom.

Mum: Yes, of course, please bring him.

Ròtìmí: (cooing)

Akándé: Yeah, that's fine. I think we can pause for now.

(gadgetry click)

Mum Interview #1. Pause time 01:10:13

Chapter 18

As I looked out the window of the plane, making our intercontinental journey from Europe to Africa, I became afflicted with homesickness. It had been so long since I'd left my native home, and I couldn't wait to share these roots with my son, Ròtìmí. My mind wandered back to the first time I left Nigeria for England. I was young, still in my teens, and full of hope and ambition. Now, over a decade later as we journey into the 2020s, little did I know that my journey would be filled with many ups and downs, and that I would be forever caught between two worlds.

My tenets of faith and mantle of morality have been a guiding light for me. Faith in myself, faith in others, and most importantly, faith in a higher power. Getting shot and being diagnosed with Brown-Séquard syndrome almost overshadowed the joys of fatherhood. But it was faith and months of therapy that sent my hampered, partially paralysed body into recovery. I refused to give up. I saw my faith as a seesaw, where faithfulness was on one side, and faithlessness on the other. I knew that if I could stay faithful, the seesaw would tilt in my favour, and I would overcome the illness. Thanks to a strict daily diet and regular exercise, doctors said that I had now achieved about ninety-five percent recovery. There were a few symptoms every now and again, but they were few and far between.

As I sat on the plane with Jọlá, Shẹ̀wà, and our son, I was filled with excitement and anticipation. We were on our way to Lagos, to visit my family and give Ròtìmí a connection to his heritage. As we discussed our plans for the trip, we also talked about identity. I knew that my son was too young to understand these complex issues, but I wanted to make sure that he grew up knowing as much as possible about his African and Black heritage.

As we talked, we were joined by my old university professor, Professor Ọkafor, who had been eavesdropping from the seat behind us on our conversation about African identity. We dived deep into a discussion about the struggles of being Black or African and living in diaspora. We talked about the importance of unifying as Black people, and how Pan-Africanism can help us achieve that. We also discussed how a Black person in Africa is not just a Black person, but a person who is divested from race categorisations and the influences of white supremacy.

We also discussed code-switching as a survival tactic and the contentious debates surrounding African hair, often referred to as nappy hair. We delved into the revisionist history of enslaved and indigenous people, analysing reparations and repatriations as a path to long-term reconciliations. We touched on the civil rights movement and how it opened doors for many, as well as the issue of corruption across the African continent and the optimism of a brighter future. We also discussed the beauty of African hospitality, culture, and innovations.

As the plane descended into Lagos, we parted ways with Professor Ọkafor, grateful for the new insights and perspectives he had given us. I know that there are many challenges that come with being British and having a Nigerian heritage, but I am grateful for the richness of experience it has brought to my life. I am proud of my African ancestry, and I know that it is my responsibility to pass that pride and knowledge down to my son and future generations.

As we stepped into the airport arrivals, the familiar faces of my stepdad, Mum, and Dámi greeted us. I dropped my bags at my feet and wrapped my arms around my parents; I hadn't seen my stepfather since the day he dropped me off at the same airport years ago. Some part of me always felt like my stepfather quietly resented me all these years for not returning to Nigeria. But even if he did, the smile on his face dispelled any such speculations of a grudge towards me. My mother gracefully stooped, gently raising Ròtìmí from the ground, and commenced anointing him with oríkì praise poems, as his cheeky smile gave the impression he understood every word of Yoruba he heard. Shèwà and I exchanged a swift, knowing look, as we shared similar adoration for our son in the moment. Jọlá's eyes lit up as she spotted Dámi waiting for her. They embraced each other tightly, lost in their own world of sisterly love. I watched with joy as they walked away together, hand in hand, towards Dámi's car. We had agreed that Jọlá would stay at Dámi's apartment for the first few days of our trip. The bond between the two sisters had grown stronger; it was heart-warming to see how close they had become. Jọlá's confidence had grown immensely over the past few years too, and it was evident in her demeanour. Once plagued by self-doubt, she had now blossomed into a beacon of self-assurance, bringing me some respite that her frequent behavioural therapy sessions had yielded such positive results for her. The rest of us went into my stepdad's car.

"Don't worry, everyone, I'll bring Jọlá over to the house in a few days. We have some catching up to do," Dámi said, as both sisters giggled away while struggling with Jọlá's baggage.

As if she suddenly remembered something, Dámi turned around and said, "Also, AK, don't forget we have that design review meeting with the watch manufacturers in person this week. It's an important one, you know."

"No worries, I'll be ready for it. Thanks for setting it up!" I responded as I waved at her.

As I looked over at the siblings walking away, I was proud to see the stronger emotional connection between the sisters and also a deeper mutual understanding clearly on display. I hoped this blossoming co-dependency would create an unbreakable bond between the sisters as they helped each other heal from their shared trauma.

When we got to our parents' home and settled into our rooms, my mind shifted to another matter that had been weighing on me and that I'd wanted to discuss with my mother. I searched around the big house for her, looking around and getting used to the atmosphere of the new place. My stepdad and mum had only moved into this home as recently as two years prior. I saw framed pictures of them, me, my younger brothers, my grandparents, Aunty Mimi, and lots of other relatives hung up on the wall. I took my time with each of them, trying my best to guess where and when the pictures were taken. I kept moving across the picture collage until I finally saw my mother through the window, bent over in the garden, tending to some plants. As I strolled through the kitchen to reach the garden, my attention was captivated by the fridge door, adorned with intriguingly familiar fridge magnets – they evoked memories of the ones my grandpa had collected during his travels. They were probably the exact same ones. *Tokens of a lost era.*

In the garden, I walked up to my mum, admired her plants, and asked if she needed any help. She accepted my offer to help, and gave me a few instructions on what to do.

"Mum, I've been thinking," I said hesitantly. "About your legal battle to reclaim your British citizenship…"

My mother's face tightened slightly, and I could tell she was reluctant to discuss the matter. "Sure," she said carefully. "What about it?"

"I think you should consider pursuing it again," I said firmly. "It's not right that you have to go through all that trouble of visa applications because of an identity theft. You were a victim, after all. And having a British passport would make it so much easier for you to travel and visit us in London."

My mother shook her head. "Akándé mí… I appreciate your concern. But I'm content with applying for visas with my Nigerian passport. As long as I can still travel and visit my family, I don't see the need to go through more legal battles. Plus, I just got a two-year visa extension, so I'll definitely be able to visit again soon."

I could tell she didn't want to discuss the matter any further, so I dropped it. But it still bothered me that she had to go through so much trouble because of someone else's actions.

"No worries, I won't bring this up anymore," I said.

"That's fine. I do appreciate the concern, though…" she said quickly, as though she had something else on her mind. "Oh, and by the way, Ìyàbò's kids have been asking for you. Will you be able to come along with me to go see them at some point this week?" she asked.

"Absolutely, I'm looking forward to seeing them now. It's been such a long time. Shẹ̀wà, Jọlá, and I are going to see my dad on Thursday, so does Friday work?" I responded.

"Friday should work perfectly; I'll make the necessary arrangements."

That night, my brothers Wálé and Ẹnítàn came over to the house, and we all had a delicious dinner while catching up on lost time. Afterwards, we settled into our rooms. I tucked Ròtìmí into his bed and recited the usual prayers we always said before bedtime. He was a curious child, always asking questions and eager to learn new things, while I tried my utmost to keep up with the best answers. A profound swell of adoration surged within me. I looked at him, his innocent eyes gazing up at me as I nudged him to close them and go to sleep. I knew that he was the best thing that had ever happened to me. As I kissed him goodnight, I whispered, "I love you more than jollof."

"I love you more than plantain," Ròtìmí responded as he chuckled and then yawned.

In a moment of self-reflection and deep thought, I whispered to him, "A time will come when you will no longer need me. If ever that day comes, I hope I would've done everything I can possibly do for you as a father."

Ròtìmí looked at me like I had said something funny and said, "Don't worry, Daddy. I will always need you."

I smiled, got up, turned off the light, and left the room. I couldn't refrain from thinking about the father figures who had shaped me into the man I had become. My own father, my stepdad, my grandfather, Uncle Taj, and the many other men who came before me, all taught me right from wrong directly or indirectly – through their various imperfections – leading me down the path of insight. I hoped that I could be the same kind of positive influence on my son, shielding him from negativity and guiding him towards the right choices. I knew that I would sometimes make mistakes, but I prayed that I would never fail my son. I wanted him to be proud of me, just as proud as I was of him.

Once ready for bed, I placed my dream journal and my second notepad, which I referred to as my gratitude journal, on the nightstand next to me. I wrote down a number of things I was thankful for in the gratitude journal and then closed it, letting out a deep sigh as I settled into bed. The hours-long flight from London to Lagos had taken its toll on both of us, and I could feel the exhaustion in every fibre of my being.

As I closed my eyes, I heard a rustling sound and turned to see Shẹ̀wà holding her belly, her face contorted in discomfort, sitting up in the bed. "Are you okay, babe?" I asked, concern lacing my words.

"It's probably just jet lag," she replied, before rushing to the en-suite bathroom to vomit. The sound of retching made my own stomach churn.

As she emerged from the bathroom, I held out a glass of water for her, which she gratefully took. I couldn't stop myself from speculating if there was more to it than just jet lag, as she had exhibited similar symptoms when she was pregnant with our first child.

I didn't want to jump to conclusions, so I said nothing and simply told her goodnight as she returned to bed. Hoping that she would feel better in the morning, I closed my eyes and drifted off to sleep, the sound of crickets outside the window lulling me into a peaceful slumber.

The next day, as Shẹ̀wà and Ròtìmí, and I walked past the familiar bustling streets of Lagos Mainland, a surge of emotions washed over me. It had been years since I last visited

Nigeria, and seeing the place where I grew up brought back a flood of memories. The old buildings and familiar landmarks were still there, but there was also a progressiveness that I couldn't ignore. My wife, Shẹ̀wà, and son, Ròtìmí, were beside me, taking it all in with wide-eyed wonder.

— ∞ —

As we approached my old primary school, I couldn't resist the urge to take a closer look. The gate was closed, but we could still see through the barriers. Children were running around and playing in the playground. It was a strange feeling, like looking back in time and seeing myself as a child. Shẹ̀wà noticed my expression and asked, "What's on your mind, babe?"

"I was just thinking about how much this place has changed. It's strange to see it all from this perspective," I replied. But as I looked around, a thought sparked in my mind. "I've got an idea. Give me a few minutes."

I dashed off to the gate entrance of the primary school and asked if I could see someone at the guidance counselling office. I knew one used to be in the school from long ago. The security guard at the gate was friendly but unyielding. Despite my telling him I was an ex-pupil of the school, he said he only allowed people in with appointments while school was in session. So, I began calling names of teachers from my era that I hoped still worked there. "How about Mr Sàkà, or Miss Uju, or Miss Zainab?" One of those names made his eyes widen.

"Wait here," the security guard said.

Within minutes, a lady who I definitely recognised and hadn't aged since the last time I saw her began to approach me.

"Hello, Miss Zainab."

"Hello, sir, how can I help you?" she said very respectfully.

"I used to be one of your pupils. My name is Akándé, Akándé Jímòh. You taught me in my moral instruction classes, and you were my tutor in Primary 5B. You always used to say I would be a great orator."

"Ah, Akándé, how you've grown. I do remember you. So, did you become one? An orator, I mean?" Miss Zainab asked.

"Oh no no, I work in software design as a UI/UX designer, and I run a wristwatch business with my cousin, although I do plan on using my voice recordings for a project in the future, so maybe I won't be a complete let-down to you in the end," I said, with a hint of self-ridicule and sarcasm.

"You were never a let-down. Glad to see you. How can I help you?" Miss Zainab asked, shifting the tone of the conversation quickly beyond pleasantries.

"I'm here with my wife and young son." I pointed over to Shèwà and Ròtìmí, who right on cue waved back. "I was hoping I could get the school's textbook recommendations or curriculum for children his age. He will soon be four years old, and because we live in the UK, I want to ensure that his education is supplemented with learning local literature, African history detached from colonialism, and social studies – much like what I learned here as a child. That independent and experiential nature of education I got from here shaped my reasoning in numerous ways. I would appreciate the help."

Miss Zainab paused for a moment, as though she was trying to play back everything I had just said in her head. "Okay, wait here," she said as she walked off.

Still standing at the gate, I turned around, and I could see Ròtìmí busy pointing at the children and asking his mother questions about the games some of the kids were playing on the playground. There was a longing in his eyes to join them.

A few minutes passed, and Miss Zainab headed back with recently printed sheets of paper and handed them to me through the opening of the gate. "This is a comprehensive list of compulsory book recommendations, according to the Federal Ministry of Education, for the entirety of the primary school years one to six, for all subject areas. Also, there are some bookshops and websites listed on the back that can help you get the specific books you're looking for. I hope this helps?" At this point, I was smiling ear to ear.

"Miss Zainab. This is more than enough; I am more than grateful." I thanked her and the security guard, while she nodded in acknowledgement and waved to Shẹ̀wà and Ròtìmí as I went to join them across the road where they were standing.

Shẹ̀wà asked, "What was all that about?"

Then I handed her the sheets of paper for her to peruse, while saying, "Book recommendations for Ròtìmí's supplementary learning."

We continued our walk down the street. We passed by the construction site where my grandparents' home used to be, and I was swept up by a pang of sadness. The house had been demolished a few months after it was sold, and I missed the feeling of familiarity and comfort it provided.

"It's sad to see the old house gone," I said to Shẹ̀wà in an unsettled tone. "I had so many memories there."

"I know, babe," she replied with a sigh. "But things change. We have to learn to move on and make new memories."

I nodded, knowing she was right. But it still hurt to see the place where I had spent so much of my childhood gone. I began to drown in a pool of longing. But then Ròtìmí pointed out an ice cream shop just down the street, and my wife suggested we take a break and indulge in a sweet treat.

As we approached and entered the shop, a shop attendant at the door greeted us with a friendly smile. The sound of children laughing and the smell of fresh waffle cones filled the air. The shop was small but welcoming, with colourful decorations and three people behind the counter, who were attending to other customers. One of the attendants was free; he was much older than the others. He looked like a manager who just happened to be helping out because of how busy it was getting. He was a friendly-looking, middle-aged man with horn-rimmed glasses, and he stuttered slightly as he asked my son what flavour he wanted. Ròtìmí excitedly screamed "Pistachio!" and I couldn't help but smile at his enthusiasm.

Next, the ice cream man turned to my wife, who requested a combo mix of butterscotch and vanilla. Then, it was my turn to choose. I was hesitant at first; I hadn't had ice cream in a very long time, plus I was trying to keep a strict low-sugar diet. But as I looked around the shop, I suddenly had an overwhelming sensation of nostalgia and chose a flavour that reminded me of the ice cream I used to have as a child.

"Three scoops of chocolate, please," I said, pointing at the ice cream through the transparent frozen countertop display. The smooth swirls of the chocolate ice cream were hard to miss, even without the bold flavour labels. The ice cream man handed me three big scoops on a cone. As I lapped up my ice cream, my taste buds relished in the pleasure, and I shut my eyes to savour the exquisite flavour. The velvety texture and sweetness were a nostalgic reminder of my childhood. My wife and son observed me with playful amusement, as I opened my eyes after being entranced in the moment. The ice cream had the power to whisk me away to simpler times, and I was grateful for the trip down memory lane. As we made our way out of the shop, I took a pause, suddenly spun around, waited

for the ice cream man's gaze to meet mine, and uttered, "Thank
you, Mr Bassey."

Epilogue

Tòbí sat in his grandmother's living room, the afternoon sun casting a warm glow over everything in the room. He held a copy of his newly published book, *Father-Time Continuum*, in his hands, still in awe that he had accomplished his lifelong dream of becoming an author. His grandmother sat across from him, her eyes overflowing with pride and joy. Tòbí felt grateful for her unswerving support throughout his writing journey.

"Why was the placeholder title not retained, and changed from the original title of *Faith-Time Continuum* to *Father-Time Continuum*?" his grandmother asked, curiously.

Tòbí took a deep breath, ready to explain his thought process. "I wanted to highlight the themes of fatherhood, forgiveness, guilt, love, mental health, and identity that were prevalent in the book, and of course the tapes. While faith was an important part of my great-grandfather's life, I believed that *Father-Time Continuum* captured the essence of the story more accurately."

His grandmother smiled, nodding in understanding. "That's a good spin on it. Good job, Tòbí," she said, her voice filled with pride.

The journey to publication had not been an easy one, and Tòbí had faced his fair share of criticism and doubt along the way for his creative liberties, from family and book critics alike. Irrespective, the modest sales and occasional disparagement did not discourage him. Instead, it only fuelled his passion for writing even further.

Gazing at endless rows of greenhouses lined up in the barren fields outside his window, Tòbí still wrestled with his fascination for writing and using his agricultural expertise to combat food scarcity in his community. Then again, maybe he didn't need to choose one. Maybe he could do both. Maybe he could do it all. But ultimately, he knew that following his passion was the right choice for him. He had chosen the path that brought him the most joy and fulfilment, even if it might not be the most lucrative.

Tòbí's decision to persevere with his dreams and preserve his great-grandfather's stories was a courageous act of self-discovery. By immortalising Akándé's legacy in *Father-Time Continuum*, Tòbí had ensured that his great-grandfather's stories would live on for generations to come, by inspiring others and providing a window into past misadventures for future enlightenment.

Acknowledgements

I owe my deepest thanks to my number one fan and personal cheerleader, my amazing wife. She didn't just tolerate my endless hours of writing, but even joined my 'committee of proofreaders' – always giving me a side eye that meant, 'Stop sending more rough drafts with more changes!' Love you, wifey! Big shout-out to my unbeatable parents, whose words range from 'So proud of you!' to 'Have you eaten today?' Your wisdom, experiences, and influence shaped this book beyond measure. To all the well-wishers and 'When will the book finish?' inquisitors, your genuine motivations kept me going. Can't forget the Almighty for inspiring me and making this a therapeutic writing process. I hope this is as freeing for you all as it is for me. Cheers!

Introducing Tósìn Akọmoláfẹ, a talented author making his debut with this captivating novel *Father-Time Continuum*. Born in Lagos, Nigeria, Tósìn now resides in the United Kingdom with his family. His educational journey took him to esteemed institutions like Kings College Lagos for secondary school, Babcock University where he pursued a degree in Biochemistry, and Queen Mary University of London, where he further honed his skills with a postgraduate diploma in computing and information systems.

Beyond his academic pursuits, Tósìn has always had a deep passion for literature and cinema. As an avid reader and film enthusiast, he actively seeks out films that have been adapted from books. This passion sparked his desire to write as a hobby from his teenage years. Drawing inspiration from the art of adapted screenplays, Tósìn brings a unique perspective to his storytelling.

Website: www.tosin.uk
Instagram: mr_syno